THE SIGN OF A WARRIOR

LEANNE HILLS

Published by Pearson Education Limited, Edinburgh Gate, Harlow, Essex, CM20 2JE.
www.pearsonschools.co.uk

First published by Pearson New Zealand
a division of Pearson New Zealand Ltd
67 Apollo Drive, Rosedale, North Shore 0632, New Zealand
Associated companies throughout the world

Text © Leanne Hills 2013
Original edition edited by Lucy Armour
Original edition designed by Sarah Healey
This edition designed by Sara Rafferty

The right of Leanne Hills to be identified as author of this work has been asserted by her
in accordance with the Copyright, Designs and Patents Act 1988.

First published 2007
This edition published 2013

17 16 15 14 13
10 9 8 7 6 5 4 3 2 1

British Library Cataloguing in Publication Data
A catalogue record for this book is available from the British Library

ISBN 978 0 435 14436 4

Printed in Malaysia (CTP-VP)

Acknowledgements
We would like to thank Bangor Central Integrated Primary School, Northern Ireland;
Bishop Henderson Church of England Primary School, Somerset; Bletchingdon Parochial
Church of England Primary School, Oxfordshire; Brookside Community Primary
School, Somerset; Bude Park Primary School, Hull; Cheddington Combined School,
Buckinghamshire; Dair House Independent School, Buckinghamshire; Glebe Infant
School, Gloucestershire; Henley Green Primary School, Coventry; Lovelace Primary
School, Surrey; Our Lady of Peace Junior School, Slough; Tackley Church of England
Primary School, Oxfordshire; and Twyford Church of England School, Buckinghamshire
for their invaluable help in the development and trialling of the Bug Club resources.

Every effort has been made to contact copyright holders of material reproduced in this book.
Any omissions will be rectified in subsequent printings if notice is given to the publishers.

A division of Pearson New Zealand Ltd

Contents

one

"Ash! It's your dad."

Gran turtles her neck round the door and I nearly take her out on my way down the hall. She smiles at me as I snatch up the phone. "Dad, how's it going?"

"Great. I'll be back in a couple of days. Sorry you couldn't come with me this time."

Not as sorry as me because, when the choice is between school and parachuting into a game park, what can you say? It's not that I've got anything against the ancient Greeks, and the Olympics are great – that's what we're studying now at school – but hunting for bush tucker is more my kind of thing. That's what we did last time I helped Dad with one of his stories. We dug up honey ants with an old Aboriginal guy who had grub-like fingers and pot-scrubber hair.

"Ash, I've got some exciting news. Remember that magazine I did the cover story for last month?"

"Sure."

"Well, they want me to do a feature for them in Africa."

"Africa!"

It's a magic word that transports me to a deep, dark, lion-infested jungle, where drums are beating and the men with spears held high are as black as bat wings …

"This could lead to a whole lot of new opportunities for me," Dad breaks in.

For us, I'm thinking. I'm dangling between an adrenalin rush of excitement and some pretty scary thoughts – like facing a lion with only a pointy stick and a tea towel tied around my …

"Ash?"

"Sorry, I was just thinking about what a great time we're going to have. Africa – unreal."

There's a silence. It's that same silence you experience when you're floating through the air just after you crash your bike.

"Ash, it's going to be a long trip this time and

… well … you're just too young for this one."

And down it all crashes – me, the spears, the men and the jungle. A torrent of baboon and lion noises rains around my ears.

"Make up your mind, Dad. Last time I wanted to go with you, you said I was getting too old to take time off school! And now …"

"Look," Dad interrupts, "we'll talk about it when I get home, okay? Can you put Gran back on please?"

I hold the phone out from my ear like it's the cause of all my problems and think about drop-kicking it down the hall. But the fight just kind of trickles out of me as I stare at a photo on the wall of me and my parents, waving from a boat.

"Okay …" I answer, my voice dawdling and hanging around for excuses while I think of something else to say. I can't come up with anything, so I just say, "Bye, see you soon."

Gran's looking worried when I hand the phone back to her.

Africa! He's got to let me go with him. I can't take any more of being left behind while he has adventures. So I step into my thinking shoes, walk up some inspiration, and it slaps the smile back on my face. I know what I'll say – I'll tell him that I'm not just a kid and that I've got what it takes. The two of us, we're a team.

With a pitch like that, I reckon we could even get sponsorship. Our own T-shirts – *Ash and Dan: real men on real adventures* – and a whole range of Action Ash toys. I'm buzzing as I go into my room and look over the photos of me and Dad for the millionth time. There's a wall full of them, documenting our escapades. In one I'm leaning up against Dad's Landcruiser, its white paint blasted with fine red dust. There's another of us in the rainforest – a pair of human icy poles melting in the heat

I let the photos talk to me, and I can feel my buzz disappearing. If he doesn't take me with him, I'll die. I'll shrivel up like a snail in the desert sun. Missing out on the last game park was one thing, but a long overseas trip is completely different, and it sounds like it might be just the first one. He might be gone for months at a time, or only come back briefly between jobs.

I lost Mum. I can't do anything about that, but I'm not giving up my dad without a fight.

A couple of days later, when I get up for breakfast, Dad's door is closed. He's home and resting. I stare at the door, shut against my impatience, and decide to let him sleep. It takes superhuman effort.

Gran's sitting in the kitchen, staring out the window with her hands wrapped around her favourite mug like somebody wants to steal it. I take her mind off her thoughts. "Morning, Ash. I guess you've seen who's here?"

"Yeah, what time did he get home?" I ask, pretending I'm not that interested.

"I don't know. I didn't hear a thing."

That's surprising, because she would usually wake up if a spider tiptoed across her room wearing bed socks. Dad, on the other hand, could sleep through a stampede of grandmas at the opening day of a knitting needle sale.

"I guess he's tired. We'd better let him sleep," I say. But I'm no good at waiting. It's genetic. Like Gran on Saturday nights, hoping her lotto numbers have finally come up. Actually, I think she might have a gambling problem because, when the lottery draw is on TV, she can't speak – she just grunts if you make a noise, and pulls a face like a sheep with bellyache.

"Yes, and don't you go *accidentally* waking him up, either."

"As if I would do anything like that," I say, *accidentally* slamming the fridge door shut. While she makes another cup of coffee, I finish off my cornflakes as fast as I can. Eating soggy cornflakes is like trying to swallow wet toilet paper – I know what I'm talking about, because I did that once when I was two years old. Suddenly, the kitchen door swings open and Dad swaggers in.

"Ah, Daniel, good morning. Sleep well?" Gran asks, reaching for Dad's coffee cup.

"Morning, Mum. Hi, Ash, how's it going?"

"Great," I say, leaping up from my seat. Then I sink back and drop my head, remembering my whole future is dangling by a thread. I need to play this right.

Gran pours Dad's coffee into the cup she keeps for him. It sits on a shelf while he's away. I imagine the bowl I use every morning – the one with Peter Rabbit on it – sitting next to his cup when we're off in Africa.

Dad sips his coffee slowly. He's not with us, he's still wandering between his last trip and sleep. He looks like a bear that's been pulled out of hibernation and put through a carwash, with his fluffy black bathrobe and his hair sticking up everywhere. I can see he could do with some hugging, but there's a table and a you-left-me-behind space between us.

"So, Ash, what did you get up to while I was away?"

I stop my tongue saying, "Thinking up ways to convince you to take me to Africa", because it's all about how you play your cards. First, you string the other person along. "Nothing much," I answer. "How was your trip?"

"Great. You remember that community we stayed with in central Australia last year?"

Now I bluff a little to lead Dad on. "Sure I do. It was something else, sitting around campfires listening to Aboriginal people tell stories in their own language. A life-changing experience, really." I'm reeling him in, I can feel it.

"Mmm, well, I'm thinking about combining material from this last trip with pieces from that one and writing a longer piece for the magazine."

Just before he gets suspicious, I use the old element-of-surprise trick and ask, "Great. So, when do we leave for Africa?"

Gran looks at me like I've said a rude word, but Dad just puts his coffee cup down and grins back. "Ash, you never were one to beat around the bush."

"Runs in the family!" Gran snorts.

"Well, Dad, you're always saying that there's no better way to learn about a place than to go and see it for yourself."

I have him right where I want him. Gran might be able to beat me at cards, but this time I'm on a winning streak.

"You're a sharp one, I'll give you that," he says, swallowing the last of his coffee.

"That's what comes of raising a kid to think for himself," says Gran, nodding.

"You can talk, Mum."

I can feel it coming on – one of those weird adult moments when they go all mysterious and a kid's on his own. Then Dad looks at me. "You know things will be very different over there. I'll be staying in a Maasai village, so there'll be no electricity or running water."

"As long as I get to see a real live lion, I don't care if we can't wash for a month."

"Why doesn't that surprise me?" Gran says.

She's probably just as worried about Dad going as she is about me, but she can't say anything. Dad's big enough to make his own mistakes.

"I guess we'll have to check with your teacher first," he says, giving me a wink.

The wink puts him on my side. It's always a bit of a juggling act – me, Dad and Gran. We're three very different planets caught in the same universe, never quite plotting the same course.

Just as I'm thinking my life's been saved, I remember the one giant obstacle – my teacher. There's a chance she might persuade Dad that it's not a good idea for me to go, which is why I've been working on a plan. On Monday morning, I'm going to try the travelling-broadens-the-mind argument. I stole it from Dad and teachers love that stuff.

And Gran – well, she'll come around to the idea. I am, after all, her only grandson and therefore entitled to truckloads of spoiling.

"You all right, Ash? You look like you're on another planet," Dad says.

"I am," I say. "Planet Africa."

All I can think about are hippos and spear-carrying warriors – and me and Dad in safari suits. Two modern-day explorers, on the adventure of a lifetime, with not a splash of soap or a maths test in sight.

two

My teacher was a pushover.

As soon as I told her about going to Africa, she went all starry-eyed and started reminiscing about her trip there a few years back. She talked about the people she'd met, the colour of the sunsets and markets she'd visited.

"Hey, Ash," Dad calls from the kitchen, "good news. I've just been to see Miss Rawlings and she thinks the trip's a really good idea."

"Cool," I call back, as I walk to the kitchen from the TV room.

She worked magic on Dad.

"She's a *really* nice lady," Dad says, his eyebrows jumping up and down like a couple of raccoons on a trampoline.

I'm about to remind him that she is in fact *Mrs* Rawlings, and that he'd better not get any ideas. The thought of him and my teacher together makes me feel like decorating his boots with chewed-up peanut butter sandwiches. That would be a waste, though, because they are my absolute favourite, especially if you throw in some raisins and BBQ crisps.

"You okay, Ash?" he asks, slinging his backpack over a chair before diving into the fridge.

"Sure," I say. "So, it's official. Just you, me and deepest, darkest Africa."

"And the billion other people who live there."

"Do you reckon we'll see any lions?"

"What is it with you and lions?" Dad asks as he pours himself a big bowl of blackberry yoghurt. "Remember that dream you used to have?"

"Yeah, sure."

When I was little – just after Mum died – I had dreams. I can still remember them clearly. I'm in the middle of the jungle and everything's oversized. The leaves look like umbrellas. It's dark – not because it's night-time, but because the jungle's so dense that it won't let in any light. Then I hear it. Every time it's the same sound, curling around the vine-tangled tree trunks – the roar of a lion.

Dad left the light on when I went to sleep for nearly a year after the last of my lion dreams. I was only a kid then, with a runaway imagination. These days, I'd give anything to see a real, free-roaming lion. Well, that's what I decide in the bravest part of my mind.

"Hey, Dad, what would you do if you met a lion in the jungle?"

"Run like the wind."

"Seriously?"

"I don't know," he says, yoghurt smeared all over his whiskery chin. "I think it's the kind of thing where you don't know how you'd react until it happens. It would certainly separate the men from the boys."

"The men from the boys?"

"After an experience like that, you'd know what you were made of."

In the part of my brain that often gets in the way of my most fearless thoughts, I see a small boy staring into the darkness, a scream caught in his fear-frozen throat.

"I was only little when I had those dreams," I say, not sure who I'm trying to convince. "I'm twelve now."

"Not quite," Dad reminds me, wiping his chin with the back of his hand.

"In sixty-two days I will be."

"But, hey, who's counting?" he sniggers.

I give him the look I've been perfecting for a year. It says: you only find this funny because your funny bone was removed at birth. It seems to be working, until he bursts out laughing again.

Talk about insensitive. I'd report him to the Centre for Children's Healthy Self-Confidence, if I knew their number. Except maybe I wouldn't, because he's not too bad if you look at him as a package deal.

Besides, if I turned him in, they might not let him take me to Africa, which would definitely scar me for life.

I've just discovered one of the most disappointing facts of life – adventures need preparation.

First, there's the paperwork. I need a passport, and for that I need a serious photo, but somehow, every time the flash goes off in the photo booth, I manage to pull a face like Aunt Julie does when she's plucking her eyebrows. Dad said I was still recognisable, which I think was meant to be a compliment. I'm still making my mind up on that one.

After the passport, there are the visas. Millions of forms and more photos. I'm going to use some of the silliest shots, the ones that aren't any good, for my passport. They'll give the embassy staff something to laugh about between coffee breaks, and they seem to have a lot of those because they're hardly ever open. Dad says they grow lots of coffee in Kenya, which probably has something to do with how many breaks they have.

Kenya. I've been letting that word roll around in my head for a week now, but not much has stuck to it, so I've decided to hit the library to see what I can find out.

By the way, there are no tigers in Africa. The librarian is smiling at me like I'm losing my mind because I asked her why I can't find any tigers in the books on Kenya. What I want to do with the books right now is drop them on her head. But she's taller than me, so I just say, "I'm actually going to Africa in a week."

"That'll be nice," she says, squinting. You can tell she doesn't believe me.

But what's the use in arguing with people like that. I'll bet the furthest she's been is the shelf holding the books on China and that her idea of taking a risk is bringing back a DVD two weeks overdue.

This hasn't been a confidence-boosting week. Today, Mrs Rawlings made me stand up in front of the whole class and tell them about our trip. I went as red as a pair of seagull's legs and could hear a chorus of "As if", until Mrs Rawlings said, "Ash's very talented father told me that they will be staying in a traditional Maasai village."

After that, even the kids I haven't spoken to since I was eight years old started asking me questions. It was like I'd been born in Africa, not down the road like everyone else. I told them about the coffee bean growing and the lack of tigers and realised that the Kenyan

Information Centre won't be offering me a job any time soon.

I've run out of time to go back to the library, so I'll just have to find out what Kenya's like when we get there. And why baboons have shiny red bottoms. One of my friends asked why – I'll have to send him a postcard when I find out.

Needles! I'm not a wimp or anything, but over the last week I have been treated like a human pincushion. Hepatitis! Cholera! Yellow fever!

The doctor kept making jokes about the size of the needle – right up until he stuck the thing in my arm. I fantasised about what he'd look like with a syringe stuck in his nose. Dad told me that if you think of something nice it helps with the pain, but the syringe-spiked nose image definitely worked for me. As if the injections aren't enough, we're also taking foul-tasting pills.

"So, Dad, what are these for, anyway?" I ask, as he sorts through his stuff for the trip.

"Malaria."

"What's that?"

"It's a disease you catch in some parts of the world if you get bitten by mosquitoes."

"Can't be as bad as these pills," I say, chucking the bottle in the air and catching it in the hood of my jacket.

"One day you'll knock yourself out doing stuff like that," he says, shaking his head like he's never done anything dangerous in his life. "Believe me, these pills aren't so bad. Malaria can be fatal."

"Lucky we don't have it here, then. Some of the mosquitoes in Gran's backyard are as big as eagles and, if one of them bit you, you'd be dead in thirty seconds flat."

"Lots of people die from it in Africa because they don't have the money to buy medicine," Dad says, putting his First Aid kit into his pack.

"That's terrible. We should take some extra pills with us in case we meet any sick people."

"Ash, it's more complex than that."

And I know it is, but it annoys me anyway. Like the time when I was little and I didn't want to finish my dinner. It went like this:

Gran: "Think of all the poor starving children in Africa."

Five-year-old me: "We could stick it in a parcel and send it to them."

Gran: "It's not that straightforward. Just eat your greens."

Stuff like that really gets to me. Why can't we just pick the world apart and put it back together in a simple way, so that you can hold it in your hand and it makes sense.

But then, maybe life's all about eating your brussels sprouts.

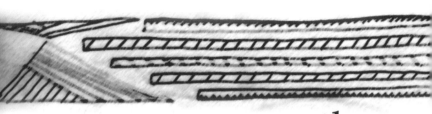

three

"Hey, Ash, I need your passport!"

"I know it's in here somewhere," I say, going through my backpack. Dad's eyes are burning lava pits into the back of my head.

"Ash, I …"

"Here it is!"

I hold it up triumphantly, with my best don't-leave-me-in-the-lost-luggage smile, and hope I don't get the document lecture. That's the one hat always ends with, "Lose your passport and you're a goner." It's true. Without your passport you're like a soldier without his dog tags – unless your gran sews your name on everything you own like mine does, including my underpants!

"Good. Here's your boarding pass. Window

seat, non-smoking. So, no buying cigars in duty-free."

"Thanks, Dad, but I'm cutting down anyway."

That's a standard Dad joke – the kind you have to remind yourself to laugh at. But then I'd rather think about Dad's joke than the look on Gran's face.

"Oh, Ash," she says and grabs me.

She smells good, like biscuits fresh out of the oven. The kind of biscuits I get my hand smacked for trying to steal before they're cool. I let Gran hug me for a while, then she lets go and stands back to look at me, as if for the last time. I feel Gran's gaze undoing me.

"Bye, Gran. We'll miss you," I say, but I'm already gone.

Me and my backpack are drawing a direct line to Departures.

"You okay?" asks Dad, joining me. He, too, is swallowing back sadness at leaving Gran.

I try to say "sure", but it gets strangled halfway out. The lump-in-the-throat thing is blocking its way. We've been vaccinated against everything but that.

It's cool how from a plane the whole world looks like a model train set, complete with built-in weather systems.

"Ash, do you know that we'll be going in the opposite direction to the planet? So, although the flight takes ten and a half hours, we'll be arriving only four and a half hours after we leave."

"Wow!"

"That's why people get jet lag – because their body clock gets all confused," Dad explains.

I've never thought about my body having a clock that's just ticking away in there, like those old blokes who've got pacemakers to keep their hearts beating in time.

"Ready, Ash?" Dad asks, looking as excited as I feel.

Across the aisle from him is a woman who's only just managed to squeeze into her seat. She's burrowing for her seatbelt and I think it looks like trying to find a chunk of melting butter in a stack of pancakes. A kid leaning over the back of the seat cheers when the woman finally fishes out both ends of the seatbelt and buckles it up.

As the plane takes off, I look out to see Melbourne's swimming pools turn into blue sparkling dots, and watch my world shrink till it's just mashed potato clouds.

~~~~~~~

It's night when we reach Africa.

We're in Harare, the capital of Zimbabwe, and this is our second stop, because we took on fuel in Perth. It's too late to fly to Nairobi tonight, and as we trudge down the rickety steel staircase on to the tarmac I get my first whiff of Africa – the air feels humid and smells of dirty socks washed in diesel.

Then I notice that nearly everybody else is black, which is logical, but I still can't help feeling a bit out of place.

"Dad, everything's weird."

"Don't worry, Ash. Jet lag, remember."

"I know, but it seems more than that."

"Probably a bit of culture shock, too."

Which makes sense because it feels like shock treatment – like I've been shaken loose from everything that holds my world together and dumped into a meteor shower, where things keep bumping into me.

When we get to the hotel, I'm still dodging stuff. I try to keep my eyes open, but they seem to have disconnected from my brain during the flight, just like everything else.

My head lands on the pillow and even that smells of Africa. In my mind, I form a picture of Gran and my room back home and hope that when I wake up things will hold still.

Nairobi airport is like a circus.

The only thing missing are the elephants and, because I'm in Africa, I expect to see one at any moment, checking in his trunk.

Some people are dressed in western clothes, but most look like they've been invited to a fancy dress party with a technicolor theme. One thing's for sure, Dad and I are definitely outnumbered. For the first time in my life, I'm noticing the colour of my skin, and people are staring – at me.

Not everybody's looking at me. It's mainly women wearing wildly patterned dresses and bits of material around their heads. Dad says they're from West Africa, from places like the Ivory Coast and Senegal. Places that I've never even heard of before.

A lady wearing particularly colourful clothes, carrying about fifteen bags on each arm, is waddling over, holding out her hand like she's going to pat me on the head. I move behind Dad before she can get close enough to touch me.

"What a lovely boy. Is he your son?"

Dad smiles at the woman and moves aside, leaving me completely exposed to her dimply hand. Luckily, it's busy rearranging her bags.

"Yes, this is my son, Ash."

"He has beautiful white hair."

The woman looks like she's about to drop all her bags and rugby tackle me just because I'm blond.

"Ah, Dad, I think our luggage has arrived," I say, dragging him behind me and whispering in his ear, "We'll have to sort out this whole father-son-travelling thing before things get out of hand."

"Whatever you say, Ash," Dad says, with his usual smile.

All of our luggage is there, but as we haul

it off the conveyer belt we can see that it has been opened. Dad warned me about stuff going "missing" in transit and showed me a special trick – you put dirty washing on top. The person hunting for something to take gives up before they find anything good. My dad knows about all the important things in life.

I put a pair of underpants at the top of my pack. I'd worn them at gym class for a week and road tested them on Gran. She nearly passed out and said a word I'd get grounded for saying when she opened my pack to check I had my comb.

Combs are a big thing in Nairobi – I've seen a few guys walking around with them stuck in their hair. Maybe it's in case a talent scout looking for dandruff advertisement models spots them. Or maybe it's what girls here find cute. I'm not sure which, but so far those are my most likely theories.

At Customs they let us go straight through – after a Customs officer has finished patting me on the head. I'm definitely going to have to buy a hat, preferably one with large spikes.

I calm down at the Currency Change counter, where we cash in our traveller's cheques for

Kenyan shillings, or *shilingi*, as they call them. For each dollar we get stacks of shillings, which is a pretty good deal. Dad hands me five hundred shillings, broken up into smaller notes. "This is so you've always got some of your own money. Just in case."

His comment sends me off on a voyage of possibilities … Just in case I get lost in the jungle and come face to face with a bunch of cannibals? Somehow I think I'd be better off walking around with a bag full of chicken wings. Just in case.

"Let's go," Dad says, heading for some big swinging doors with *Welcome to Nairobi* written above them. We're not even outside when a group of men swarm around us, like a flock of seagulls at a park swooping on a dropped chip.

"Hey, Mister. I have best taxi. Very cheap, very fast."

"No, Mister. He cheat. My taxi good, no problem. Come, come."

Dad smiles and keeps walking. A guy grabs hold of my backpack. I'm stuck like a beetle, my arms waving in the air. Dad's heading for the doors, and the men are circling and closing in on me.

four

"I know good hotel, not expensive. Hot water all day."

Here I am struggling even to breathe and all the guy can think about is hygiene. That's when Dad turns around – I guess he finally heard me screaming his name. He gives the guy a look I've never before seen on his face and it works a treat. Good looks run in our family.

Putting his hands in the air to show he wants a bit of space, Dad says, "Thank you, gentlemen, but we've already arranged transport."

With that the taxi drivers are off like a shot, flocking to a tourist who looks like he's just seen a herd of deranged wildebeest stampeding his way.

"You've already organised everything?"

"I haven't, but at least it got that lot off our backs."

What a guy! He's in his element while I'm just gulping for air. As we walk towards the Accommodation counter, a guy comes over to us. At first I only notice his super-white teeth as he grins at me, but then I do a double take. His earlobes look like they've been pierced with a baseball bat and, even weirder, he's pulled them up so they hang over the top of his ears, to keep them out of the way.

"Hello, my name is Robert. I have a taxi if you would like to go to the city."

Dad stops and answers him. "Hi, Robert. Yes, we would like a taxi. How much do you charge?"

Dad and Robert negotiate a price, while I just stare at those elongated earlobes. Robert sees me gawking and unhooks them to show me how big the holes are – the fat end of a baseball bat would certainly fit into them.

"In my village we wear very big earrings," he says, laughing.

"I can see that," I say, joining in. His smile carries you along. It takes you on a ride.

"Ash, Robert's going to take us into town, and he knows a good hotel where we can stay."

"Cool, let's go!"

A few taxi drivers try to intercept us on the way out, but Robert speaks to them in his strange-sounding language and they soon disappear.

"He's speaking Swahili," Dad explains, as we get into Robert's taxi.

"Swahili?" I ask.

"It's the common language here, along with English, but most people speak their own tribal language as well."

"Robert, what's hello in Swahili?" Dad asks.

"*Hujambo*."

"*Hujambo*? That's easy."

It sounds like jumbo, which makes me think of Dumbo the elephant, and all of a sudden I'm entranced by Robert's ears again.

"Here's something you should learn if you're going to stay in Kenya for a while," Robert says. "*Hakuna matata*."

"Hey, I know that. It means 'no worries'." I know it from *The Lion King*. The theme song starts up in my head, until something catches my eye.

Running along the edge of the road, on the other side of a fence, is a giraffe! It's tilting backwards and forwards as it goes, like its long legs can't bend enough to let it break into a sprint. It's like a rocking horse on stilts.

"Wow, look at that!" I yell.

Dad smiles, rubs my head and says, "Africa's full of surprises, Ash. You'll see."

Soon the road is clearly heading into the city.

The streets fill up with people wandering around. They're buying and selling, squatting and cooking on the sides of the road. There are women wearing what look like colourful sheets. They're balancing tubs of cleaning equipment or food or hair stuff on their heads. Some of the women have babies on their backs, like koalas, except they've tied them on with bright strips of cloth.

When we stop at the first set of traffic lights, I see some kids about my age selling lighters. One's pushing them against the window, chanting "cheap, cheap", and all I can say is, "I don't smoke."

The light changes and we move on, but the kids' voices are still in my ears.

I stick my mouth into gear. "Hey, Robert. What's it like living in Africa?"

"I don't know," he says with a grin, "because I've never lived anywhere else. Here we are."

We've pulled up outside a square blue hotel. There are palm trees around the entrance and a froth of bright pink flowers grows against the walls. I go to get my backpack, but Robert stops me. "Let the porter take it."

"It's okay. I can carry my own stuff."

"I'm sure you can, but it's the porter's job."

The look on Robert's face lets me know it's the right thing to do. Dad starts to pay Robert for the ride, but I don't want him to go, so I whisper in Dad's ear, "Can't you get him to show us around a bit?"

"Yeah, good idea."

Dad and Robert have a quick chat and then, rearranging his ears again, Robert comes over to shake my hand. "So, I'll see you tomorrow."

"Cool!"

"*Hakuna matata*."

Something about Robert tells me that life for

him is pretty much *hakuna matata* every day of the year. In fact, the whole place has that kind of a feel. Like you could turn up to school in your pyjamas and everyone would just say, "Hey, dude, looking good." A woman walks past wearing only a skirt.

"You okay?" Robert asks, climbing back into his taxi. "You're as red as a baboon's bottom when she's looking for a man friend."

"And as good looking as one, too," Dad says, with a laugh.

So, now there are two things on my mind. One: I know why baboons have bright red bottoms, although I'm not sure how I feel about that. And two: I'm wondering if Nairobi has a branch of the African Society for the Prevention of Cruelty to Children because Robert and Dad seem to be ganging up on me.

When Gran talked about Africa being dangerous she probably meant the food.

Breakfast is cardboard cornflakes, fluorescent pink jam and milk that tastes as if it's straight out of the cow! I'm sticking with bananas.

Dad's reading the paper, being really boring, so I bite off the biggest piece of banana I can stuff in my face and try to say, "Me Tarzan."

"You look more like Cheetah to me," he says, laughing over the top of his newspaper.

I try to say something smart back, except my tongue is plastered to the bottom of my mouth.

"Robert's picking us up in about half an hour and he's going to help me make a few contacts. He's a Maasai, you know."

Managing to swallow the sticky banana mess, I ask, "That's who you're doing your story on, isn't it? The Maasai?"

"Yeah and Robert thinks he knows a village where we could stay."

The Maasai are famous warriors who kill lions to show their strength. The bravest warrior gets to keep the lion's mane and wear it as a hat at ceremonies, which must get kind of heavy and smelly. I'm wondering about wearing a dead animal on my head when Robert shows up, so I go straight to the point. "Hey, Robert, have you ever killed a lion?"

He beams one of his huge smiles at me and

puts his hand on my shoulder. "You know, today we Maasai aren't allowed to kill lions. They are protected by the government."

"But what about all that warrior stuff? Isn't that how you prove your courage?"

"A man has many ways of proving his courage, Ash."

I feel sorry for Robert. It must be really difficult to change the way you live because of someone else's rules – especially when you are a warrior. It's probably why he took up driving taxis.

I try to imagine him all dressed up with a spear and a shield, baseball bat-sized earrings hanging off his ears, and me standing next to him: Ash, the first white Maasai warrior, key-ring-sized and ready for a fight.

We spend most of the morning touring around the city, visiting contacts Robert has lined up for Dad and doing a bit of shopping. I feel lost.

I told Dad I'd be all right with Robert if he wanted to go off and organise a few things on his own, but he decided he'd rather stick with me. I think Gran might've given him a lecture about not taking his eyes off me when we got to Africa, because the only time I get any privacy is when I need to go to the bathroom.

They don't have price tags here, so you've got to haggle for everything. If you're not careful, you can get seriously ripped off.

An old guy, whose skin looks like an elephant's with a bad case of eczema, is standing outside a souvenir shop selling weapons, masks, shields, wooden figurines and stuff. I whisper to Robert that I'd like to buy a wooden figurine of a lion, so he promises to help me haggle.

I try a line that I heard once in an old gangster movie and put some hustle in my voice. "So, how much do you want for it?"

The old man screws up his face and looks at me through folds of ancient skin. "Five hundred shillings."

Five hundred shillings! That's all of my "just in case" fund. I look at Robert, but he just nods calmly and says, "We'll give you one hundred and fifty shillings."

A look of horror spreads over the old man's face. "This is a good model – it's hand-crafted.

Four hundred shillings."

"It is a good model, but we can't give you more than two hundred."

Robert is smiling at the old guy the whole time. This is a game with a whole set of rules I can't figure out. It's looking tricky when all of a sudden the guy puts the model in my hand and says, "Two hundred and fifty shillings, last price. Very cheap."

Robert nods to me and I stuff the model into my backpack before putting the shillings into the old man's hand. He counts the notes carefully and puts them into his bag then, raising his hand to his head, he toddles off down the street.

"So, did we get a good price?"

"We got the right price."

"How do you know?"

"The look on his face."

I didn't see any look on that old guy's face that said what price to pay, so I figure warriors just know things. Like how to walk down a busy street in Nairobi without snagging your ear holes on telephone poles.

five

I'm hanging out the window of our room the next morning, watching the world go by – well, the African part of it – when Dad says it's time for us to head downstairs.

"Ash, I'm going to meet some more contacts Robert has set up for me this morning and, with any luck, we'll be leaving for a Maasai village in the next couple of days."

"Robert's village?" I ask, heading out the door.

"Don't know yet. We'll see."

"Maybe I'll be able to score myself one of those lion hats if I get lucky?"

"Headdresses, you mean. You never know."

"Hey, why don't you go by yourself today? Robert can take me to the market. He told me about an old shop he'd like to show me."

Dad looks kind of hurt. "Wouldn't you rather come with me?"

"Yeah, sure," I say. But Dad's meetings are kind of boring. "I don't want to disappoint Robert, though. Anyway, I'll be okay."

"You sure?" he asks, probably wondering what Gran would say.

"*Hakuna matata.*"

Dad laughs and I can see I'm winning him over, so I add, "Don't worry, I'll translate for you when we get to the village."

"Nice idea," he says, heading down the stairs. "The only problem is they speak Maa, not Swahili."

I'm wondering how anybody manages to get a conversation going in this country, with all the languages they speak, when we meet Robert coming the other way, his elongated ears swinging to and fro.

"Hey, Robert."

"Hey, Ash."

We shake hands. Everybody around here does a lot of hand shaking – either they slide their hand across yours without really taking hold of it, or they take hold of it like they'll never let go. I haven't discovered yet what each handshake means, but I'm working on it. Wondering about things like this gives me something to do when Dad's so buried in his pile of maps, you'd need a compass to find him.

~~~~~~~~~

Robert and I leave Dad at a hotel where he's got a meeting with some Maasai men and we go through packed streets to the main market.

It feels good to be out alone with Robert, but it isn't easy keeping up with him. The only thing that seems to slow him down is saying hi to just about everybody he goes past. He even says hello to one of those "dentists" – you see them sitting on the footpath with their rusting tools, waiting for a patient. I take a closer look and decide the rust might actually be dried blood. The guy's grinning at me with half a mouthful of teeth, and I can feel mine beginning to ache.

"He fixes my teeth," says Robert and shows me a crater in the back of his mouth. I make a secret pledge never to touch chocolate again in my life.

The market is buzzing and I attract eyes like a magnet – something to do with being the only white kid around. A couple of times I feel fingers in my hair.

It's in a rickety building, with a huge area in the middle open to the sky, and there are people everywhere, balancing bags, tubs, jerry cans and bucketfuls of water on their heads. It's like they're doing a kind of dance – things stay suspended in the air as their hips sway around.

I'm thinking about how hard it must be to keep an idea in shape with all that weight squashing on your brain when one of the fruit sellers waves to Robert, then to me.

"*Hujambo*, Moshobi," the guy says to Robert.

"*Moshobi*?" I ask, confused.

"Moshobi is my Maasai name. Robert's my school name and it's better for business."

Robert speaks to the guy in Swahili, but every now and then I hear my name so I know they're talking about me. I just grin and focus on my little toenail – they must think I'm stupid, because nobody in Kenya speaks only one language – not as far as I can tell.

Just past the fruit and vegetables is the meat.

The air is filled with a rotten smell and the buzz of frenzied insects. As we go past, butchers hack off chunks from carcasses hanging up on big hooks. An old woman pays for a sheep's head, complete with eyeballs, and a side serving of flies.

But worst of all are the dried fish laid out on long tables – the smell is like being buried alive in a sardine factory. Robert just laughs when he sees my face. "Come on," he says. "The shop we're going to is upstairs."

I follow him up and along the open corridors, until suddenly he stops in front of a small shop in a corner, nearly hidden behind the jewellery and the masks.

He beckons me in. It's dark after the bright sunshine, and so packed with things we can hardly move. As my eyes adjust to the gloom, I feel like Ali Baba minus the forty thieves. Every kind of African treasure is stacked up around me, most of it disguised in dust. From behind a pile of drums, a voice bellows something in Swahili and Robert moves in its direction, with me hanging off his shirt.

Sitting on a wooden stool is an ancient man. He's so dried up, you could mistake him for one of the animal skins draped everywhere. Robert speaks to him in a hushed voice and I'm getting the same kind of vibe I got when we went to church after one of Gran's friends died. A word comes creeping out of the dust – it's "sacred" and that's how it feels.

The old man looks at me and says, "Welcome, young man. Moshobi says you are interested in Maasai weaponry."

He sounds like wisdom and he's even wearing a cloak, so I say, "Yes, sir," even though I've never called anybody "sir" in my life.

"My name is Odinga. Come with me."

Odinga gets up and walks to the back of the shop, all in a kind of slow motion, while Robert signals for me to follow. Behind a curtain is another room, smaller and more sombre, and Odinga lights a candle so that we can see.

As the space becomes clearer, I can make out what's hanging on the walls. There are shields made of animal skins and long spears with points tied on neatly with strips of leather, next to some gruesome-looking clubs and necklaces covered in beads – all of it ten times better than anything I've seen people selling on the streets.

But best of all are the masks and hats made of feathers and different types of skin.

Then I see it, and the universe shifts. Hanging there, right in the middle of everything, is a lion's mane.

"Ah, I see you like the lion headdress."

Odinga takes it down off the wall and then it hits me – the lion's smell trapped in its mane. I can almost feel him in that tiny room with us and the hair stands up on the back of my neck. Whoever wore the headdress would become like the lion.

The light from the candle makes Robert's eyes protrude from his dark face. He's smiling at me. "I told you it is a good shop."

I want to say something but I can't think of the right words. Odinga presents the headdress to me and I put it on my head, just to feel what it's like. But my neck strains under the weight and its scent goes up my nose and curls through my veins.

As I hold both hands up to balance it, I get the feeling that something important is happening – significant for me, but even bigger than that. I've suddenly understood something, even if I can't wrap it up in words or give it a name.

Then the other side of my brain starts up and says maybe it's the weight of the headdress squeezing my thoughts in all directions, because, after all, it's only a hat. I take it off and hand it back to Odinga. All I can say is, "Thank you."

"You're welcome, young man," he says, hanging up the headdress. "You can visit my shop any time. A friend of Moshobi's is a friend of mine."

I hesitate for a moment. I'd really love to have one of those headdresses, but now I wonder whether or not it's something that you buy. Then my dream comes back to me – the silence of the jungle broken by a roar. And the lion drawing closer. I can almost see his face.

As we head back out into the light and noise of the market, I can't quite shake off the memory of that dream. This place is really starting to get to me. I'm not sure if I'll ever be the same again. Maybe that's why Gran looked at me the way she did at the airport, because she knew the old Ash would never come back.

I realise that, for the first time in my life, the thought of changing doesn't really frighten me. Change isn't always a bad thing.

six

Dad's meeting was a success and a couple of days later we're ready to hit the road.

Our new driver is leaning out of a four-wheel drive with more dents in it than a can that's been kicked along a street. This driver will take us to Maasailand. Robert won't be coming with us – he only drives taxis in Nairobi.

"Hello, my name's Henry."

He looks a lot older than Robert, and I'm just thinking he seems a bit too old to be driving people around when he says, "There's not much I don't know about this place. Anything you want to know, ask me."

To find out whether or not Henry's bluffing, I ask him a question I already know the answer to – "How fast can a cheetah run?"

Henry doesn't look fazed. "A hundred and ten kilometres an hour, in short spurts."

"Ready, Ash?" Dad asks, chucking our packs in the back, on top of lots of plastic sacks. "I see you've met Henry."

"Sure have." I can see the old guy going into gloating mode so I switch subjects. "What's all that stuff?"

"Mainly camping gear for the national park, and food to take out to the village. Can't turn up empty-handed, now can we?"

"Guess not. You didn't tell me we'd be staying in a national park."

"It's a surprise. You can't go to Africa without going on safari."

"Cool. But I'm not sharing my tent with any wildlife."

"Don't worry, Ash. The only thing you'll be sharing a tent with is me."

My dad snores sometimes, but at least he doesn't bite. "What about Henry?"

"He's got his own tent."

"The animals are my friends," Henry says. "On cold nights they are welcome in my tent, except of course Mister Porcupine! He is not a good bedfellow."

"Yeah, right!"

Henry finds the whole thing incredibly funny and soon tears are pouring down his face. Dad and I just look at each other, as if to say, "It's going to be a long ride."

As we drive off, Henry notices the necklace hanging around my neck.

He grabs hold of it to take a better look and nearly runs over some poor guy running across the road with a huge sack of footballs balanced on his head.

"A royal tooth," he says, looking impressed.

"It's from Africa," I say, tucking it back in under my T-shirt.

"So you've been to Africa before," says Henry.

"Actually, Ash's mother and I travelled around Africa before he was born," Dad tells Henry. "She bought this lion's tooth in case she ever had a son."

Dad's gone quiet, but my jaw's on my knees. He never told me that before – about it being a present from my mother. Something inside me wonders why I never asked. I pull it out again and squeeze it between my fingers. It makes me feel comfortable, a special kind of safe.

"It will protect you," says Henry. "It once belonged to a king."

And all of a sudden I feel completely invincible. But having Dad and Henry along for the ride is okay – even superheroes need sidekicks.

~~~~~~~

Henry just can't stop talking for a moment.

This wouldn't really be a problem, except that he doesn't take much notice of anything else once he gets stuck into a story, including other traffic, or which side of the road he's on.

"Hey, Henry. How come Nairobi's the capital of Kenya? It's a long way from the sea."

"Ah, that's easy. Nairobi was built because white men needed a town on their new railway line between Uganda and the coast of Kenya. They called it Nairobi from –"

"Ah, Henry, there's a guy on a bicycle up there and I think he's kind of deaf because he's not moving over!"

Henry just laughs and honks the horn about fifty times, till the guy moves over into the dirt, collecting two goats and a prickly bush on his way. I'm thinking you'd have to be a crazy lunatic to ride a bike on these roads, but Henry doesn't even blink. "They called it Nairobi from the Maasai name that means 'the water which is cold'."

Dad's hand is on the dashboard. "That's very interesting, Henry, but there seems to be a herd of cattle up ahead there. Maybe you should slow down."

"No problem. Plenty of room."

Henry leans on the horn again until I can't hear myself think, then, at the very last moment, when I'm sure we're going to crash, he swerves. The car bounces up and down as we hit the dirt, then pulls just as fast back on to the road, veering to the other side of the herd of cows.

Henry looks pleased with himself. "I told you. No problem. Not one scratch."

Dad's kind of out of it. He likes four-wheel driving on tough terrain, but not with live obstacles.

"You not scared of old Henry's driving? I never had an accident."

He has to be joking, what with all those dents.

"Yeah, but have you killed anything?"

"Not really."

"What do you mean, not really?" I ask, suspiciously.

"One time I just missed a big truck, but he lost control and drove into a family of goats."

"A herd of goats," says Dad, not looking very impressed.

"Yeah, you never *heard* such a big noise in your life when that truck went smack." Henry laughs so hard he almost drives into a mud hut that somebody has built too close to the road.

"Maybe I should drive for a while?" Dad suggests.

Suddenly, Henry looks worried. "Oh no. It's far too dangerous."

He's serious but, when Dad and I crack up, Henry just shakes his head and says quietly, "You white fellows have strange humour," while everything else in a five-kilometre radius cringes and ducks.

~~~~~~~~

It's starting to get dark when we arrive at the campground. The area is covered in long dry grass, with just a few trees scattered about. It's like a lot of the land round here. There are already big groups of tents set up, and people sitting around campfires talking and preparing food, but – just my luck – there are no other kids.

We all work together to get our tents up as fast as possible in the remaining daylight and then, while Dad unpacks, I go over to give Henry a hand with dinner. He's busy cooking things in pots and some steaks are already sizzling on a grill.

I feel a small sting on my hand and look down to see a mosquito sucking away at my blood. As I go to squash it, it zings away into the night and I'm glad that we're taking those malaria pills, even though they do taste like envelope glue and unripe lemons all rolled into one.

All you can see in the darkness are the groups of people glowing in the light of their campfires, but what's giving me the creeps is what you can't see – maybe a lion or two checking out our dinner from the shadows, or even a couple of leopards hiding up some trees?

"The animals do not like fire," says Henry, looking at me, his teeth lit up in his shiny face. "Anyway, you're too small for a lion's dinner. And I'm too old and tough."

He laughs so hard he nearly falls off his stool. One thing's for sure, there's no way I'll be getting out of my tent to go to the toilet, even if I have to lie there with my legs crossed till dawn. I'd rather miss out on a few hours of sleep than end up being something's midnight feast.

seven

The only lion that visits my tent during the night is the one in my dreams.

Except this time, it's not so much jungle in my dream, but grasslands, and the one thing I can see clearly are its eyes, bright and piercing in the darkness.

As soon as it's light, I stick my head out of the tent to make sure the coast is clear and make a quick run for the toilet. I hate pit toilets and these ones smell like a pile of week-old dirty nappies. It's cold enough to freeze the warts off a cane toad, so I jump into my sleeping bag as soon as I get back, which wakes up Dad.

"You're up early."

"Had to go to the toilet. Man, do they stink."

"Yeah, I know. I'd rather squat in the bush any day," he says, yawning.

"Me, too, although you've got to be careful what you're squatting on around here. I swear I saw lion tracks on the way back."

"Ask Henry. He'll be able to tell you."

Just then the tent starts moving and I figure something must be after an early morning snack. "Get up, lazy bones. Time to go on safari."

Henry. Lucky he didn't do that in the middle of the night, or he might've ended up with a tent pole stuck between his eyes.

For breakfast, Henry fries eggs and makes flat bread on a big piece of round metal. "*Chapattis*," he says, handing me one.

It's good, though a bit dry. Dad rolls his eggs up in one and makes a real mess trying to catch the drips with his tongue. We love camping, getting dirty– we're in our elements.

Henry's keen to get going before the other groups set off. "I know the best places. I don't want the other groups following and making noise. It's very important to be quiet. We don't want to scare the animals away."

Scare the animals! Somehow I just can't

imagine an enormous elephant getting nervous over me or Dad, and the only thing that might frighten them about Henry would be his driving or his jokes.

Before we leave, I go back over to the tent and check it's zipped up. I don't fancy getting back later and finding a lion in my sleeping bag.

Henry shouts, "Let's go!"

Henry and Dad are in the front, so I climb up on the back seat and poke my head out through the big sunroof. It's hard to hang on because the track is really bumpy and I'm feeling like a rodeo cowboy riding a horse with hiccups. I holler out to Henry, "Hey, slow it down a little or I might lose my breakfast up here."

"No problem. Can you see any animals from there?" he asks, speeding up.

Animals? I can hardly see the road. I'm about to change position when the car comes to a halt and I land backside first on the back seat. Henry's pointing madly out the window. "Look!"

Dad and I both strain to see what he's talking about, but there's nothing but long grass. Then the grass starts to move.

"What is it, Henry?"

"Ssh, it's a mama with her babies."

Dad pulls his binoculars out of his pack and tries to focus on what Henry can see. "I don't believe it."

"What? Give me a go."

Dad hands me the binoculars. The first thing I see is a long tail sticking up from the grass, like a submarine's periscope, then the mother and her three cubs suddenly become clear.

"Cheetah!"

I watch as she walks, sniffing at the air, checking out if there's any danger around. The way her muscles move you can tell she's built for speed. Like an Olympic sprinter. Henry's ready with his usual bits of information. "She has a back like an elastic band. That's why she can run so fast."

The cheetah is like a giant spring, set to take off. Her cubs look like little kittens, but somehow I know she won't let me take one home for Gran.

Then she sticks her nose in the air and decides that we aren't safe, giving her cubs a quick lick to turn them around. Her cubs follow her tail through the grass like the Japanese tourists I once saw back home, following their guide's umbrella.

"Wow! I didn't think we would find animals so easily."

"In case you didn't notice, Ash, we didn't find them. We would never have seen those cheetahs without Henry's keen eye."

"No animal fool old Henry."

Sometimes I just can't help myself – "Not even a cheetah. Get it? Cheetah, cheater?"

Dad groans, even though it's his fault I think like this. Between him and Henry, I don't have a chance. Henry starts up the car again and we head off into the long grass, following a track that's really well camouflaged. The savannah stretches out all around us like a big yellow blanket with a couple of folds in it. The only wildlife I can see is birds.

"See over there," says Henry after a while, pointing to some big chunks of rock with a few trees around them. "Good place to find lions."

"Hey, Dad, chuck your binoculars over."

I stand up on the back seat again as Henry pulls over and turns the engine off. At first I don't see anything, but then I catch movement at the edge of my sight. High above us, sunning himself on top of the rocks is a large male lion. He gives a big yawn and shakes his mane, like he's just got out of bed to take a pee.

I hear a rustle in the grass, right next to the car, and I look down, down into the eyes of a lion. The hairs on the back of my neck bristle, just as they did in Odinga's shop, and I try to imagine what it would be like if I was down there in the long grass, just me and that lioness licking her chops. This reminds me of my dream – my nightmare – and, all of a sudden, I feel five years old again, frozen in the agony of my fear. That's when I realise that the sunroof is big – large enough for her to get into.

Henry whispers, "Don't move."

I almost laugh because I'm having trouble budging anything more than my lungs, which are pumping in jerks. The lioness is staring into my eyes. I see the muscles in her shoulders tense up, and I feel something rise in me. It could be panic or it could be courage, but she doesn't give me the chance to decide.

With her gaze locked on me, the lioness steps

forward, and I'm sure she's going to pounce. Then, abruptly, she turns her back on me and disappears into the long grass. I drop down on the back seat. Henry takes one look at my face and cracks up laughing. "No problem, Ash. If you don't move, the lion doesn't attack." Then he adds more seriously, "But you run, you lose."

All I can think is that now I know why they call a group of lions "a pride" – that's the proudest looking animal I've ever seen. I, on the other hand, am feeling like Einstein would have if he got a D for his maths test – though, come to think of it, didn't he fail maths?

"Hey, look. There's another one."

Dad's pointing out the window in the opposite direction and suddenly Henry's face drops as he spins around. This time it's Dad's turn for a laugh. "Fooled you."

Henry's look of shock turns into an oversized grin. "You guys are really funny. Anybody want to have toilet stop?"

For some reason, nobody says "yes".

It's pretty dark when we get back, because we stayed out as long as possible to watch animals coming to a waterhole at dusk.

Even though Dad's wildlife list is two notebook pages long, he's keen to add a leopard, but none turned up for a drink.

One of my favourite bits of the whole day was watching giraffes eating leaves off thorn-covered acacia trees. They must have rubber lips, because it looked like they were munching on a bunch of roses wrapped up in barbed wire.

For dinner, Henry's rolling up some strips of meat and tomatoes in *chapattis* – kind of African-style wraps. He's put tins of condensed milk in the embers to turn into caramel, which he'll pour over sliced bananas. That sounds better than good.

Dad is making notes and looking up birds in his ornithology book. I stare at the fire and think about the pit – the one that's replaced my stomach since we saw the lioness. The pit's the size of a crater and feels like it's full of quicksand – the kind that sucks objects in and never spits them out.

I wake up in the middle of the night to the sound of a lion's roar.

Or maybe it's just another dream. But, in this dream, I'm holding a spear that keeps shrinking, while the lion licks its chops.

Worse thing is that I need to go to the toilet, and badly. I lie snuggled up in my sleeping bag for a while, trying not to think about it, but it doesn't work.

Then I have a brilliant idea. I'll pee into my drink bottle and empty it out in the morning, which sounds kind of disgusting, but in the bush, survival comes first.

I grab hold of my backpack, but my bottle still has some water in it, so I open the zip of the tent to tip the water out.

"Ash, is that you?"

"Yeah. Sorry, Dad, I'm just pouring some water outside."

"What for? Is it morning?"

"No. But I need to go to the toilet, so I'm going to pee in my drink bottle."

"You can't do that. Afterwards it'll be

all contaminated. Hang on a minute." Dad wriggles his top half out of his sleeping bag and starts pulling his jumper on. "Come on, I'll take you to the toilet."

"I can probably hang on till morning."

"It won't take long. Now you've woken me up, I need to go, too."

I throw on some clothes because it's freezing outside, and we take torches, because the moon is hidden behind some clouds. I can hear movement from the different groups of tents, and one even has a light on in it, but beyond that it's all blackness. My torch beam stretches a little way up as I point it skyward, but gets gobbled by the night.

One bonus – the toilet doesn't stink so much in the cold. I go first, but I leave the door open – half because of the smell, which is what I tell Dad, and half because you never know. Then it's Dad's turn.

I keep my eyes on the patch of dirt I can see in my torchlight, and even that seems to be crawling under my fear-hazed eyes. I hear a noise. It's coming from left of the toilet, from the other side of the rubbish pit, and I suddenly realise what an inviting place it must be for half-starved wildlife happy to eat anything in sight. I throw back my panic and cup my hands in the direction of the toilet door, which I now see is closed. "Dad? There's something out here."

Dad's torch is disco dancing through the gap between the door and the ground and his voice is a rasp. "What is it?"

"I don't know. Hurry up."

He comes out of the toilet still pulling up his trousers as the thing moves again. It sounds big, and this time it's coming for us.

"Not good," says Dad, instead of something useful, like Dads are supposed to say when you're so scared you could turn inside out. I'm about to attempt a new 100-metre world record when I remember what Henry said – "You run, you lose." Just then the moon comes out from behind the clouds.

"Look, Ash!"

My dad's shining his torch right at it. It's big all right, and moving pretty fast, but this isn't a lion. It's a porcupine. It looks like some overgrown cactus that's had too much fertiliser put on its spikes.

"Is it dangerous?" I asked, imagining myself skewered, turned into an oversized kebab.

"I don't think so," says Dad, but he doesn't sound too sure. "It's not really that big. It just looks it with all those quills."

The long quills are black-tipped and wobbling. Disturbed by our torchlight, it stops dead and snorts at us, like it's saying, "This is a private dinner, and you're not invited." For a moment, I think there's going to be a fight. I'm imagining myself with more holes than one of Gran's baking sieves when the porcupine suddenly turns round and goes back to its pit. Dad and I crack up.

"Ssh, you'll wake the other campers," Dad whispers, but he's the one having trouble shutting himself up.

Me, I'm feeling kind of proud of myself. We've just survived a charge from a starving porcupine, in the middle of Africa, in the dead of night. On the scale of dangerous things, it isn't as lethal as a lioness, but, at almost twelve years old, I have time to work my way up.

eight

Henry just can't help himself.

All through breakfast, while we're packing up, and even once we get moving, he just keeps getting fits of the giggles every time he looks at us.

"How much further, Henry?"

"Further than you can throw a porcupine."

"You walked straight into that one, Ash," Dad says, rolling his eyes. "Don't worry, we should get there by late afternoon. We'll have plenty of time to set up camp."

Just then we pass some Maasai men walking beside the road. "Hey, Dad, look. Their hair's all covered in red mud."

"Ochre," says Dad.

"Oh, yeah. It looks like what the Aborigines use back home."

The Maasai men's hair is done in tiny plaits. Silver decorations are laced through the plaits, holding them together.

"How come the men do all that stuff to their hair and the women just shave their heads?" I ask.

Henry takes the opportunity to remind us that he's a regular walking encyclopaedia. "In the animal world, the male is the most beautiful. Look at the lion with his handsome mane."

"So, how come back home it's the women who spend the most time making themselves look beautiful?"

Dad smiles. "Different cultures, different ways."

"They all look so sure of themselves," I say, watching them disappear into the dust out of the back window.

"They are warriors," Henry says, serious for once in his life.

"Wish I was one," I let slip.

"Inside, all men are warriors," Henry says. His voice blends with the landscape as we speed past.

Somehow, Henry managed to keep down the number of near misses and death-defying swerves for the last part of the trip.

Although at one stage he ran over a chicken that definitely had more feathers than brains. Instead of feeling bad about it, Henry started telling some of those really old jokes – the ones that go, "Why did the chicken cross the road?" I'd like to find the tourist who taught him those and string him up by his camera strap.

"Here we are," says Henry, finally turning off down a rutted track towards some mud huts. "Enkasara."

We stop the car just outside the village and I take a look at where we're going to spend the next month. Kids, most of them smaller than me, are heading in towards the huts, which are surrounded by thick clouds of dust. Small herds of cows and goats wander around.

A Maasai man with short hair walks over to us and holds out his hand. "Welcome to our *enkang*, Daniel."

"Hello, Moses. Good to see you again."

Moses! I'm wondering what kind of Maasai name that is when I remember he probably got that name at school, like Robert. It must be handy having two names, especially if you get in any kind of trouble. You could just give them the name you don't use very often and they'd never be able to track you down.

Then the guy turns to me. "And this is your son? Welcome."

Moses shakes my hand and his skin feels as dry as a mouthful of peanut butter on a hot day, in the middle of a drought.

"Hi. My name's Ashani, but people call me Ash."

"How old are you?"

"Twelve, end of next month."

"My son is thirteen. You will be good friends."

That's nice. Except, I'm thinking, if his son isn't cool. Dad cuts in on my thoughts, "It's Maasai tradition that men and women of the same age spend most of their time together."

Moses puts his hand on my shoulder and I feel more than his words going into me. "When I was a *moran* I did everything with the other *moran*. We slept together, ate together. A *moran* never does anything alone."

Moran is their word for warrior – Robert already told me that, and for the first time I'm getting a sense of what that might really mean. I think about asking him if they also go to the toilet together, but I don't because we've just met.

"Are you still a *moran*?"

He doesn't look like one because his hair's short and curly, and he seems a bit old.

"No. Now we are elders and we have wives and children to care for, but we are still joined by our age and our position. My son will soon become a *moran*."

I decide it could be cool to hang around with an apprentice warrior. "What's his name?"

"Ranan."

As if on cue, a kid a bit taller than me comes walking towards us carrying a container on his back that looks like a long wooden mango. He speaks to Moses in a language I've never heard before.

"Is that Maa?" I ask, remembering what Dad said.

"Yes, it is, and this is my son Ranan."

The kid sticks his hand out and speaks like a

teacher has just asked him a question and if he doesn't answer correctly he'll be on detention for the next ten years. "Pleased to meet you. Welcome to our village."

I shake his hand and so does Dad. I try to see the warrior buried inside that skinny body of his – to imagine him with a spear.

"Pleased to meet you, too. What's that?" I ask, pointing to the thing on his back.

"Milk," he says, taking the container off and offering it to me.

I look at Dad and he gives me a "go for it" wink. I lift it up slowly, so as not to get a faceful, and take a sip. It's warm and tastes like cowpats, but the whole thing feels like a ceremony, so I say, "Um, yeah. Very nice, thanks."

I hand it back to him and he gives it to Moses, who passes it to my dad. Dad takes a sip, but I can't tell by the look on his face whether he likes it or wants to throw up. "Straight from the cow. It's very good," he says, handing it back gently.

The kid looks really proud of himself and I guess he's done the milking. I hope he'll teach me how.

"A man has two things he loves – his cattle and his children," says Moses proudly.

I wonder what his wife thinks about that, because back home if you said something like that, your wife might turn warrior on you and you'd need a Maasai shield to save yourself.

Moses adds, "We will soon eat. Would you like to join us?"

"I think we'll set up camp and eat over here just for tonight, but please join us later so we can talk."

Moses nods at Dad's answer.

"You should come, too," I say to the kid so he won't feel left out, which is a bit like inviting somebody to their own party, but Dad seems to know what he's doing.

"Thank you," he says and they nod at us and turn around and walk back towards the village.

"So, Dad, why aren't we sleeping in the huts?"

"Not the first night. It's better if we get to know them a little before we move in."

Sounds like a good plan. Besides, sleeping with Dad, who snores like a rhinoceros with sinus problems, is one thing, but a whole hut filled with people is something else.

I'm not sure how I feel about the mud hut, group sleepover thing. It's different now that we're actually here – I'm ricocheting between excitement and dread. And, for some reason, I feel like a nice, hot bath.

By the time we finish dinner, people are hovering around us like flies over hot meat.

When Moses arrives, the others come closer to the fire to say hello, or just listen in. Moses sits down and speaks to Henry in Swahili. I wish I could understand what they're saying.

"Henry's a Kikuyu, which is a completely different tribe, and they don't always get on with the Maasai," Dad explains.

But Henry and Moses don't look like they're about to throw any punches, and luckily there are no spears in sight. Dad goes over to talk to some men who look about his age. The men who speak good English translate for the others. Dad looks weird in the middle of a bunch of guys wrapped in red blankets who are wearing enough jewellery to sink a small boat.

Dad is wearing his usual beige shirt and matching trousers with pockets all over them for the stuff he carries around, like film and his Swiss Army knife. He only wears beige because he reckons it doesn't show the dirt.

A group of girls, about eight or nine years old, keep looking at me and giggling. I'm trying to ignore them, but they gang up on the biggest girl and push her towards me. She gets her balance back but just stands there staring and grinning. I don't know whether to feel sorry for her or tell her to bug off, so I say, "Hi."

There's more sniggering. One thing about girls is they're the same wherever you go – always carrying on and giving guys a hard time.

"Hello, my name is Matangara."

The other girls crack up. Ranan is watching us. I'm wondering whether he's going to jump in and help me out when he walks over and speaks to the girls. Whatever he says works, because they settle down and go and sit on the other side of the fire. "Matangara is my sister. She likes you."

I think I'll have to watch myself, because some tribes marry their kids off really early, and I figure

I still have a few years ahead of me before I need to worry about stuff like that. So I decide it's better to set things straight, even if it means stretching the truth a bit – like halfway to the moon and back. "I've already got a girlfriend back home."

The kid doesn't seem to get it, so I try again, this time more slowly. "In Australia, I have girlfriend."

"Girlfriend? Ah, yes, girlfriend. No problem."

I'm not sure what he means by "no problem", but at least the marriage seems to be off.

"What's your name again?"

"My name is Ranan," he says, like he's the king of the jungle. This causes a chain reaction and suddenly there are kids crowding around me, telling me their names and wanting to shake my hand. I'm feeling a bit like a movie star when Moses turns round and shoos them all away – except Ranan and a couple of his friends. Shame, I was getting the hang of being a celebrity.

"My name is Ashani," I explain to Ranan, just in case he missed it the first time round. "I was named after a monk my parents met in the

Himalayas, but it's a long story – most people call me Ash."

Ranan nods, but he seems like he's somewhere else.

As we move closer to the fire, I look over to where Dad's still sitting and talking to some men. One of them is a *moran*. He's balancing on one foot, leaning on his club. Watching him makes me wonder – is there really anything different about him, or is it just his clothes, the fire, the whole feel of where we are? Henry says that there's a warrior deep down inside all men, so what happened to Dad? Couldn't he find his?

We wake up in the morning surrounded.

Outside the tent, little voices are whispering to each other and closing in, so I creep out of my sleeping bag, open the zip, and shout, "Boo!" The little ones run off screaming, while the others slap their knees. I have the feeling that privacy's going to be a problem while we're still the major attraction in town.

Henry's going back to Nairobi today and he won't be back to pick us up for a month. A whole month in a Maasai village. No TV, no computer games, no electricity, but, then, no homework either. I can get used to that.

"So, Henry. Watch out for the chickens on the way home."

"Okay, and you be careful. Maasai houses don't have locks. Remember Mr Porcupine – not good for your blow-up mattress."

Henry's back to normal after being a little quiet around the Maasai. Moses and Ranan arrive to help us carry our stuff just as Henry's leaving.

"You are ready?"

"Lead the way," says Dad, slinging on his pack.

We walk through a gap in the enormous circular wall of thorny branches, which is there to protect the village. Inside, the mud huts are also in a circle, and at the centre of the village there's an open space with a couple of dried-up looking trees. I see smaller circles of thorny walls that look like they're meant to keep the animals in. The whole place is covered in flies.

"This is our house," Moses says proudly, stopping in front of one of the huts.

The walls only come up to his shoulders and, the closer I get to them, the less I think they're actually made of mud. There's something about the hut. It isn't quite right. I give Dad a suspicious look, but he isn't about to say anything, so I figure there's only one way to find out. "What do you make your houses from, Moses?"

"They are made from branches covered with mud and straw and … what is the name?"

Moses bends down, picks up a piece of dried cow poo off the ground and holds it up to me. "This. But fresh."

"You mean cow dung? How do you get them to poo in the right place?"

"The women put it on with their hands."

I reckon being a *moran* must be pretty cool, but I wouldn't be a Maasai woman if you gave me a truckload of BBQ crisps, and I haven't had a BBQ crisp for ages. So we'll be sleeping for a month in a dung house – I won't be mentioning that one in my next postcard to my class.

I have to duck to go into the hut, and when we get inside I can't see anything because it's so dark. Even the flies seem to be having trouble finding their way around. One of them flies right into the side of my head before taking off out the door. Eventually, my eyes get used to it and I can make out things in the little room we're standing in. Moses tells Dad to sit down on one of the stools.

Squatting by the fireplace is a woman with a shaved head. She's making tea. Ranan turns to me and introduces her. "This is my mother, Nataiya."

"Hello, my name is Ashani."

I've got used to using my full name, because people here seem to prefer it – and they don't treat me like it's weird. As Nataiya leans forward to shake my hand, I notice she has a face like one of the carvings I saw in Odinga's shop. She's got a smile you know you can trust.

"My mother is beautiful," Ranan says, which seems to me a strange thing to say to somebody you hardly even know. But he's right – she's very beautiful.

"My mother was also beautiful," I say, even though I'm not sure whether I only remember her face now from photos. Moses turns to me.

"Your mother is dead?"

"Yes," I say, swallowing hard.

I'm wishing we could talk about something else when Moses puts his hand on my shoulder and speaks in a deep voice, like Mufasa from *The Lion King*. "The death of a parent is very difficult, but it helps us become who we are. To grow stronger."

I feel a lump growing in my throat the size of a basketball and for a terrifying moment I think I might cry. Then I catch a scent of my mother and try to hold on to it, but it's gone. It's disappeared into one of the dark corners of the hut.

Ranan's standing beside me. "My mother is your mother now," he says.

Nataiya looks up from her tea and smiles at me again. I know nobody can replace my own mother, but for some reason this woman squatting by her fire makes me feel better about that.

"Ash, you okay?"

"Yeah, sure, Dad. Everything's fine."

The Maasai have a strange way of getting under your skin.

nine

Outside it's so hot my eyebrows feel like they will weld together as I squint in the sun.

Ranan is taking me for a walk around the village, or *enkang* as they call it. We visit the huts one after the other and Ranan introduces me to everybody. They all seem to be family.

"This my mother. Her name is Mumai," Ranan says, pointing to a woman sweeping out her hut with a broom made of twigs.

"But didn't I just meet your mother?"

"I have two mothers," he explains.

"Man, that must get expensive on Mother's Day. How many fathers have you got then?"

Ranan looks at me like I've just asked him the colour of his appendix and answers, "One."

How was I supposed to know? If he's doubling up on mothers, I can't see why an extra father or two wouldn't be useful, especially when you need someone to help you with your maths.

"So how many brothers and sisters do you have?"

He's doing a mental count, and I'm thinking things are seriously complicated in the Maasai family department, when finally he says, "Eight. How many do you have?"

"None."

He looks like he's considering giving me a couple of his brothers and sisters, too, when he says about the strangest thing he's said so far.

"Your father has only one wife?"

I correct him. "*Had*. Yes. Only one."

Then it finally sinks in – one of the women is his real mother and one is his father's other wife. I hope that Nataiya is his real mother. I'd pick her any day – and not just because I saw her first. There's something about the way she looked at me that made me feel like I belong, which is the feeling I think a mother should give.

Maybe he's thinking that my family tree is bare, but he just says, "Now I must work."

Visiting hour is over – just when I was starting to get the hang of things.

"What kind of work?"

"I must watch my father's cattle. You may come with me."

"Sure, why not?"

As I can't see any cattle around I figure we're probably going for a walk somewhere, so I head back to the hut to get a hat. Inside, it's like talking blindfolded because I can't see anybody, but they can see me.

"We're going to check out Moses' cattle, Dad. Is it all right if I go?"

There's no answer. I know he's there, but instead Moses' voice floats out of the dark space. "Ranan will take care of Ashani – he is older and you are our guests. It is his responsibility."

I look over at Ranan squatting by the doorway and half expect him to wink – to let me know it's no big deal and that I don't need taking care of, but he's just nodding at his dad.

"Um." I hear Dad's voice from the far side of the room.

"Don't worry, Daniel. Ranan has done this since he was a small child. Today his brother went with the cattle because Ranan wanted to show Ashani the village, but now he has work to do."

"Come on, Dad. I'll be fine. You know me – reliable, trustworthy, never get into any trouble."

"Now you *have* got me worried," he says.

Deep down, Dad really trusts me.

"Please, Dad," I say in my best how-could-you-refuse-me voice. "I don't know, sometimes I think you act more like a *worrier* than a *warrior*."

As soon as I say this, I can see that Moses isn't impressed. "Daniel has passed the age of the warrior. It is his time to be an elder – to take up wisdom and lay down the spear."

And I'm not feeling so wise right now, so I say, "Sorry," because that's how I feel.

"Okay, Ash," says Dad, and I can tell he's not angry at me. "You can go. Just take a hat with you. It's hot enough to fry an egg …"

"… on the roof of your car," I finish.

We laugh because it feels familiar, pulls us together, reminds me we're a team. I don't know if he's ever tried frying an egg on his car roof. He hardly ever washes his car, so it would be about as hygienic as eating your dinner off the street.

"Watch out for the wildlife," Dad says.

"Don't worry," I say, my eyes finally adjusting to the gloom. "If I see a lion, I'll kill it with my bare hands and bring it back for dinner."

Moses laughs. "Then you would be the bravest warrior in the village, maybe in all of Kenya."

But "in your dreams" is what he really meant, in a nice, Maasai elder kind of way.

We head out into the great African wilderness, carrying only a couple of big sticks. The land's pretty flat and is covered in long grass – good snake territory. I'm glad I've got trousers on and that I'm wearing my new walking boots. Ranan, like most of the Maasai, is only wearing a piece of material tied around his waist and sandals made out of old tyres, although his feet look so tough that a snake would probably break its fangs if it tried to bite him.

There are a few trees around – acacias, like the ones we saw the giraffes eating in the national park. The whole place looks nearly the same as the national park, except that there are big tracks where the cattle walk. I'm wondering where they keep the lions when I hear a mind-numbing scream.

~~~~~

Ranan's standing with his stick high above his head and he's ready to attack.

I'm paralysed from my big toe up. Staring down at us from the crook of a tree is a huge baboon, its mouth wide open and teeth big enough to go straight through your hand.

They say your life flashes before you when you think you're going to die, but mine's just kind of dawdling – images of all my favourite people and the things I like to eat. A slow procession of mud cakes and pizza, mixed in with Gran and my dad. And there's Mum, watching over me.

A huge noise erupts and things start to speed up. Ranan's bared his teeth and he's roaring at the baboon. He looks terrifying, waving his stick and making such a racket. I watch while they snarl at each other. I'm hoping that Ranan will come out on top.

I realise that the baboon's almost as big as me, but hunched up and very muscular. Its beard is quivering with threat. Although he's jabbing his jaw at Ranan, I'm at the edge of the baboon's vision. He hasn't forgotten me. With just this stick between my thinness and the baboon's sprung force, I haven't got a chance. I need a plan.

I flinch as I notice a fist-sized rock, but it's a move that could prove fatal, because the baboon turns on me. All that power, all that instinct is now focused on my face. My body takes an involuntary step backward, like it's saying, "I think I'll just be heading back now to do what I'm used to doing – avoiding an early death".

But something else kicks in and I roar, too. It's a little roar at first, but then I pick up the baboon's scent and dig deeper, till I'm out-snarling both Ranan and the baboon. I can almost feel the hairs growing on my chest.

The baboon keeps flipping his lip inside out, like one of those plungers you use to fix blocked drains, and the trees are filling with the sound of boys against beast. I want to look at Ranan, but my eyes are fixed on the animal. I know I can't take them off him. It's a duel – there are three of us, but only two sides. Ranan and I have become one.

Then Ranan disappears. He leaves me alone with the baboon. Fear tugs at the hairs on my neck. I've been abandoned. The trees are closing in on me and my stick, my shrinking spear. There's a narrowing tunnel between me and the baboon's sharp teeth. How could Ranan . . .

My thought is cut in half by a loud thud. All the hairs on the baboon's head shift like grass in the wind and he takes his eyes off me and spins around. Released, I look, too, and there's Ranan, poised and ready to pitch the next rock. I laugh out loud and for an instant the baboon's head swivels, twitching in my direction.

Ranan is on to it. He draws the baboon's attention away from me while I scan the ground for something to throw. I scoop up a couple of heavy stones, but hesitate for a moment, remembering a hundred "be kind to animals" lectures, then start pelting it anyway, my missiles stinging into his hide.

We are a team again. Two boy-men, working side by side in the face of the enemy. I'm darting around, grabbing stones, anything to throw. My arm soon gets into the swing of things and my body is happy with the action. Off to my side, Ranan's doing the same thing. I catch him grinning as he bends, rises and throws, over and over again.

The baboon's head is whipping between us, but I'm smaller and my weapons are lighter, so he starts his way down the branch in my direction. I see his muscles tighten and I put my stick out in front of me like a spear, braced for the impact, when there's a scream. A forest-shattering screech. A large rock has hit the baboon's shoulder. He's in a lot of pain.

His lip drops and with one almighty leap he takes off to the top of the tree. I hold my ground, waiting to see if it's a trick, but he's turned his back on us and gone into a sulk. If he had a tail, it would be tucked between his legs.

"I thought you'd gone," I say to Ranan. The feeling's still lingering, making me feel mad.

"Gone? I would not leave you," Ranan replies.

He steps towards me and as my body relaxes a series of images come crashing in – my mother's eyes, Ranan's face, the baboon's hate-filled stare. I gulp and try not to cry. This is important and I need to hang on to it. I have to do it right.

"Now I know," I say, enjoying the feeling.

"You did well," Ranan says, patting me on the shoulder. He's smiling at me and there's a mystery curling through his look. I know what it is. We've stepped closer – our paths have met – and I've just passed some kind of initiation. From the look on Ranan's face, I've scored my first A in three years. The last one was for making a unicorn in art class, which doesn't count because it was meant to be a sheep.

"Baboon," I say. It feels good to say our enemy's name now that it has been defeated. "Talk about ugly!"

Ranan laughs. "Yes, ugly, very ugly."

I look up at where the baboon sits sulking in the tree and, even though the fight's gone out of him, he still looks mean. "Ugly and dangerous."

"Yes, sometimes they attack small children and kill them," Ranan says, picking up his stick and continuing on his way.

As I watch Ranan walk off between the trees, I remember something useful I read in a book – if you ever get really thirsty, just catch a baboon and tie him to a tree. Feed him salt until he's so thirsty he could drink his own pee and then let him go. He'll lead you straight to water.

But now I've seen a real baboon – gone head to head with one – I know there's a crater-sized hole in this theory. You'd have to catch one first.

ten

As we come out of the trees into open land, it isn't hard to tell where the cattle are. The big clouds of dust that surround them make it look like they've been doing burnouts, not grazing for something to eat.

We can just make out Ranan's little brother in the middle of them and I wonder how a kid so small can control so many cows. There are at least fifty of them and they have horns the size of elephant tusks.

"My father is rich," Ranan says.

Somehow that mud hut we've just come from doesn't seem like a rich man's house, but then again I guess it depends where you're from. If I was rich, I'd buy myself some bricks rather than plastering my house in smelly cow dung.

Ranan and his brother nod at each other, then the kid heads back in the direction we came from. I don't like the idea of him running into that baboon, because he's only a little guy, but then he's got a stick and looks tough enough to scare his own shadow. Maasai kids don't get much chance to be wimps.

We sit under a tree, because it's already really hot, and let the cattle do their own thing. Luckily I've brought some biscuits, because Ranan seems to have forgotten about lunch. No wonder the Maasai are so skinny.

"Ranan, is there any water around here?"

"No. Later."

Later! Later I'll be like one of those worms you find in the garden, all shrivelled up in the sun. I'm beginning to think the Maasai aren't quite human. Maybe, like camels, they can go ages without a drink.

Catching a baboon is starting to look like a good option right now – if only I'd brought some salt with me.

After a couple of hours, I feel like I never want to look at another cow again.

Ranan has started herding them together and shows me how I can help by waving the stick, but I can't take my mind off their horns. It's like sword-fighting with fifty fat pirates who are half-blind and only say "moo".

"Now we go to the water," Ranan says.

"Well, about time," I say, feeling like a dishcloth that has been wrung out and hung up to dry.

We walk for about fifteen minutes till we reach a watering hole that looks more like something that pigs would wallow in than anything I would drink. The cattle seem to think it's good, though, and watching them is torture.

As the sun starts going down, the animals start turning up. There are zebras, gazelles, a family of baboons and a couple of giraffes. They don't seem the slightest bit worried about having us around and, as long as the baboons stay over their side of the water, it's okay with me.

"Wow, this is great."

"Our land is beautiful," he replies, as sure of that as I am of dying of thirst.

I try to imagine that the waterhole is full of caramel-flavoured milk and there aren't any stomach-eating creatures swimming around in there, but it's not working. Which just goes to show that even a hyperactive imagination can sometimes let you down.

~~~~~~~~

When we get back to the village, a couple of Ranan's sisters come out to milk the cows.

Dad's talking to Moses and looks glad to see me back in one piece. "Hi. How'd it go?"

My tongue feels like the leather earrings the old Maasai wear – the ones embroidered with beads – so all I manage to spit out is, "Thirsty."

I'm dying to tell him about going face to face with a ferocious baboon and coming out on top, or hanging out at the waterhole with the cast of a wildlife documentary that could whip up a storm. But I just keep hallucinating about lemonade, bathfuls of it, on ice.

Funny how sometimes your body just takes over. A bit like when you've really got to pee. A herd of elephants could come running through your living room and you'd hardly notice. Then again, in Maasai villages, maybe that isn't such a weird thing.

I like sleeping alone. The Maasai don't – they don't seem to do anything on their own. What's worse, there isn't enough room for both Ranan and me on my blow-up mattress, so I keep waking up face down in the dirt.

Ranan and I sleep in the main room. On the other side of a thin wall, Ranan's mum sleeps in a bed with his little brothers and sisters squished in beside her like a tin of wriggly sardines. The beds are made from bushes spread over a few planks and branches, with a big cow skin chucked on top. They don't use any pillows or sheets, just blankets like the ones they wear when it's cold.

Dad's sharing a bed with Moses just next to us and I wonder how Dad's getting on sleeping with another bloke. He explained it to me last night – how it's Maasai custom and all that – but knowing about it and actually doing it aren't exactly the same thing.

Another problem, the story of my life, is I need to pee. I *accidentally* kick Ranan so he wakes up, because there's no way I'm going on my own.

"Hey, Ranan. I have to go to the toilet."

"Come with me."

Ranan wraps himself in his blanket and, even though he's still half asleep, he leads the way. There are no toilets inside the *enkang*. Everybody goes out in the bush, where the dogs and the hyenas clean up after they've finished. Dad says they think it's disgusting that we have toilets in our houses, which is pretty weird coming from people who don't have a problem making their houses out of dung.

It's quiet outside, except for the sound of animals moving inside their thorny pens. Most of the village is still asleep. The little "mud" huts look like they belong there, along with the trees and the long grass and the birds singing in the trees. Wow, I'm starting to sound like a hippie after only a couple of days in an *enkang* – maybe my brain's still half asleep.

Outside, it's colder than camping in a fridge, but it feels good to be in the fresh air, with the sun just starting to come up. I look up to see a little monkey watching me. It keeps tilting its head from one side to the other, like it finds me the most fascinating thing it's ever seen.

Being an only child means you usually do stuff on your own, but life in a Maasai village is a group event, with all the people and animals living so close together. It's like being a member of a football team in a world full of Saturday afternoons, and never spending time on the bench.

When we get back to the hut everybody's stirring and Nataiya's already got the fire going. Dad's looking like he's just been dragged backwards through a haystack, but he's trying his best to look at home. I try to imagine Gran here but my brain won't stretch that far this early in the day.

For breakfast we have *mandazi* – which taste like doughnuts without the sugar – and tea full of milk. Then it's time for Ranan and me to get to work, because the cattle don't take days off.

"You all right to go out with Ranan again?" asks Dad as we're heading out the door.

"Sure. This is what I'd be doing if we lived here."

"It is important for children to take their position in life," Moses says, trying to be helpful, but I know Dad's thinking about what could happen out there. If I got killed, there would be no brothers and sisters to fill the gap.

He tries one last time. "You can always stay here with me." But I figure there's only one way to help him get over this: a Dad-style bad joke.

"If you like I can get you some stuff for your story – one hundred and one things to do while you're watching cows, like counting the hairs on the back of your hand."

He's laughing and nodding and I know he'll let me go, because, even though I told him about the baboon and all the animals we saw, he understands the incredible feeling I get in this wild land.

What I didn't say, because I'm still sorting through it, is what it's like to be out there with Ranan – just the two of us living off our wits and being responsible for a whole family's livelihood. The power of that trust.

eleven

A couple of days later, Dad's squatting in the shade of the hut on a blanket. All his camera gear is spread out around him like he's about to hold Maasailand's first garage sale.

"Ash, do you mind staying with me today?"

It's the first time we've been alone in ages, what with me always taking off with Ranan and Dad working on his story, and it feels good to be just the two of us again.

"Sure. What for?"

"I want to take a few photos and I could do with a hand."

My dad's a good photographer, but he's about as organised as a bunch of Kenyans trying to get on a bus with their excited chickens, mad goats and everything else. So it helps if I make sure everything goes back in the right place in his camera bags while he's shooting, and pass him filters or rolls of film whenever he needs them. He also taught me how to set up the tripod – I have no idea how he manages when I'm not with him.

"How's it going with Ranan?"

"Yeah, it's good, except it's hard work hanging round with people from another culture, don't you reckon? All that speaking clearly and not using too much slang. And there's lots of stuff that gets lost in the gap between you and them."

"I know just what you mean."

"Ranan doesn't have much of a sense of humour, either."

Dad holds up one of his filters to check it for dust. "Well, I think I know why that is."

"Because he had it removed at birth?"

"Very funny," Dad says, but he's got something else on his mind. "Remember Moses said Ranan is about to become a *moran*?"

"Yeah."

"Well, becoming a *moran* is a serious matter,

and it takes a fair bit of mental preparation."

"What kind of mental preparation?" I ask, thinking it sounds like a maths test, but a hundred times worse.

"Soon Ranan will be initiated into manhood."

"A man? But he's only thirteen."

"He'll be fourteen next month and he will be one of the first of his age set to become a *moran*. It's a huge responsibility."

"Why's that?"

"Because his age group will be judged by how well he performs during the ceremony, and how brave he is. So will Moses and his whole family."

"That's a lot of pressure to put on a kid," I say, wondering if I could handle all that responsibility right now.

"He's been prepared for it from birth. After he becomes a *moran*, he won't see his family often. He will be with the other *moran* most of the time," Dad says, adjusting one of his lenses. "They say it's the best time in a man's life."

I try to imagine what Ranan will be like a year from now, with his hair all decorated, hanging around with the other warriors. And me – I'll be starting high school at the bottom. Some warrior. Suddenly, Ranan seems like a different guy.

"Why don't we do stuff like this in Australia?"

"What, you mean rites of passage? The Aborigines still do it in some communities, but it's gone out of white culture. It's a shame, if you ask me."

"Why?"

"Well it's important to honour transition."

"In English, Dad."

He laughs and puts the lens into his bag. "I think a lot of kids back home are afraid of taking on responsibility and moving into adulthood and, when it comes to proving themselves, they do it the wrong way."

It's starting to sound like a lecture about all the things teenagers do wrong, except I know my dad did some pretty full-on stuff when he was at school, and that's not what he means.

Which makes me wonder, when it's my time, how will I prove I'm a man? For Ranan, all the questions are answered, which must feel kind of safe.

I'm waiting for Ranan outside the fence when he gets back with the cows just before sunset.

As I watch him, he seems too small to be heading into manhood, but then I guess it doesn't have much to do with size. He half smiles when he sees me and I wonder what's going on in his head. How do you prepare yourself for something so important? And, even though he knows what's coming, isn't he afraid enough to choke?

I imagine what it would be like to have my father's reputation depending on how brave I am and decide that's a very scary thought. It's a whole lot easier for kids back home, where how cool your dad is depends on which football team he backs.

twelve

A couple of nights later, a group of *moran* come wandering into the village.

They've been walkabout, like the Aborigines back home, and everyone is glad to see them and gathers round to hear their stories. I sit with Ranan, who seems very impressed.

"What are they saying?"

"They talk of their adventures. They have been travelling a long time. Many brave acts."

"Do you know them well?"

"We are the same age."

The *moran* look much older, but Moses leans over to explain. "When Ranan becomes a warrior, they will all be part of the same age set. Later they will become elders together."

Ranan is looking about as proud as you can get without exploding when one of the younger *moran* comes bouncing over like a kangaroo. "Who are you?"

"Um, I'm Ash. Who are you?"

"I am Sempuku. I am a *moran*. Why are you here?"

He might be a warrior, but he's definitely not big in the manners department. Then again, with a spear like that and all those muscles I guess he doesn't have to worry much about being polite.

"I'm staying here for a month with my father to do a story on the Maasai people."

"Then you must talk to us. Of all the Maasai people, the *moran* are the most interesting."

Modest, too, I'm thinking. The guy seems to have loads of good qualities – like being able to run his own fan club single-handedly.

"So, what's so good about being a *moran*?" I ask, because the guy's really getting up my nose. And, well, I just can't help myself.

"Everything," he says, laughing and looking back at his friends.

"Like what?"

I know this is in the running for the dumbest question of the century, but sometimes you talk yourself into a hole so deep that the sky seems just a tiny dot of blue.

"We were attacked by a lion."

"Did you kill it?"

"He was so afraid, he ran away," says Sempuku. "Only Mengoru was hurt and he has already recovered."

He points to one of the *moran* who has an enormous scab all the way down his right arm.

"That must have been pretty scary."

"We were never afraid," he says, not impressed with this line of talk.

Okay. So, don't talk to a *moran* about fear. I'll put that on my list along with "never tell a baboon he's got bad breath", especially when his canine teeth are spitting distance from your face.

"Of course. So, what happened exactly?"

Sempuku gets himself in storytelling position.

"We were walking to a village to see an *eunoto* and it was late and almost dark. We were talking about the big celebration, so we didn't hear him until he was very close. Mengoru was the last one in the group, so the lion attacked him. Mengoru is a great warrior. He is very brave. When the lion attacked him, they both fell to the ground, but Mengoru rolled over and pushed the lion away."

As he speaks, Sempuku's eyes, his whole body, tell the story for him, and he's got the crowd eating out of his hand. "Quickly, we moved towards him making noise, with our spears above our heads. The lion saw this and rose up, but then he turned and ran away. He had blood on him from Mengoru's spear. He will never forget this day."

I'll bet the lion isn't the only one who won't forget. I'm guessing that, after an experience like that, they must be pretty close friends.

"Wow. Good story."

"It is not a story. It is the *moran* way."

I'm trying, but this guy is hard to like. Ranan says something to him in Maa, but Sempuku just laughs at him. "Can't you speak English? Didn't you go to school?"

Ranan's doing his best Arnold Schwarzenegger impersonation and having trouble convincing even himself, so I blurt out, "His English is fine."

But Sempuku hasn't finished. "He is stupid and he is also a coward. He will never be a *moran*."

Ranan speaks to him in Maa and I can see he's trying to defend himself, but Sempuku just keeps on. "You see he is too stupid to argue in English. Ranan and his brothers will bring shame to the village. They have no courage and they do not understand what it is to be a warrior."

But Ranan's not done, either. "You are old. Your time is finished. It is time for new warriors."

Sempuku's face drops faster than a dead parrot from its perch. He says something to Ranan that I can't understand and goes back to his *moran* mates, looking a lot like the baboon that high-tailed it up the tree.

"Good one, Ranan," I say, happy that at least one of us has been able to shut Sempuku up.

Moses has been listening in – he's a bit of a sticky beak, old Moses – and decides to set things straight. "It is normal for *moran* to tease the boys who are soon to be initiated. It is our custom. Ranan must defend himself and show that he is not afraid."

Some custom – I'd rather chew on broken glass. I'm starting to wonder what else he'll have to go through to prove that he's a man.

"Well, that Sempuku guy's got a big head, if you ask me."

"A big head?"

"He's too proud."

Moses smiles. "You are very loyal to Ranan. You would make a good *moran*."

Loyalty and bravery. Initiations. The whole warrior thing is getting more complicated by the minute. No wonder Ranan always seems to have his mind on something else. I'm trying to work out whether to feel jealous or sorry for him when I have a great idea.

If I want to get the inside story on being a warrior, then there's only one thing to do. And it's going to take some fast-talking, juggled with the right amount of biting my tongue.

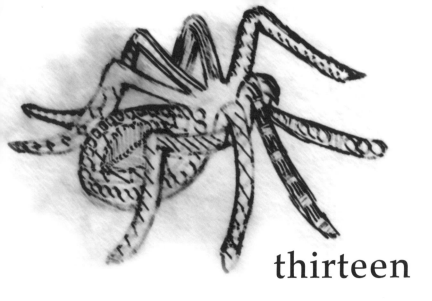

thirteen

I'm not a very good juggler and sometimes words just trip me up.

But today I'm feeling lucky, so I'm willing to give it a shot. All I have to do now is convince the *moran* that they need me on their next trip, so I'm flipping through my list of skills, trying to find something they just can't do without.

Problem is, so far I've come up with zero, so I've decided to see what emerges in the heat of the moment. With luck, a bolt of genius will strike me from the sky. It does happen. I wait till nightfall, because the darkness might help to disguise my fear and give me a dramatic edge.

Sempuku and the other *moran* are sitting around a fire, talking among themselves, when

I make my move. I take Ranan with me, even though he's not in on it – I wanted to tell him, but I was afraid he'd try to talk me out of it, and doubt's about the last thing I need hanging round right now.

The *moran* stop as we approach, like we've broken in on something secret. Sempuku's already standing and there's contempt dripping off his face. "What do you want, little white boy?" he asks, smirking at his mates.

I tell myself it's just part of the game, stirring up the younger ones, but there's something about the word "white" and the way he threw it down that makes me think he's looking for a fight.

"I have a request."

"A request?" he says with a nasty smile, and now they're all listening. "What is it you want?"

There are no lightning bolts, of the good or bad variety, so I decide just to chuck the truth in and see what comes out. "I want to go with you on your next trip."

There's silence. Ranan is staring at me like I'm pulling out my own teeth and I'm wondering whether I shouldn't have prepared him a little as moral support, because right now it's thin on the ground. The *moran* erupt into hysterics and I feel my vital organs sink into my boots.

Sempuku's grinning at me like I've just handed him a very fine gift.

"You are too young, too stupid, and you have no experience."

I'm about to say, "So far that's never been a problem for me," when I realise that my best defence is anger, and right now there's plenty of it zipping through my arteries, knocking at my temples, working its way up my vocal cords and on to my tongue. "I may be young compared to you lot, but I'm not stupid and I've done loads of dangerous things."

As soon as the words have taken the leap into the space between us, they suddenly seem less brave, more like whining, and I'm searching for evidence to back them up. Warriors probably don't think much of surviving a porcupine attack or roaring a baboon into disgrace, so I scroll through my memory for something to impress.

"At home I've been swimming where there

were sharks and I've caught a huntsman with my bare hands."

I wait to see the impact of my adventures, still rattling with anger, ready to pull out more if that's what it takes. They're talking between themselves, and I look at Ranan, but he can't make out what's going on. Then Sempuku steps forward and asks, "What is a huntsman?"

It's then that I decide that exaggeration is my best weapon.

"A huntsman is a giant spider found all over Australia. It attacks at the slightest provocation and has a very painful bite."

A glimmer of understanding begins to flicker across Sempuku's eyes, and for a moment I feel we're going to be friends. Then the arrogance returns.

"So, you are not afraid of giant spiders," he says, full of glee.

He turns around to the group and quickly says something to them that makes their chins drop to their ankles, which is not a good sign. Sempuku's attention is back on me.

"This is what you will do. Here we also have giant spiders, and now you must catch one and bring it to me. This will be, how do you say . . . your initiation. It is the way of the warrior – do you accept?"

By now my anger has had time to cool off and some of the other less inspiring emotions are creeping in, so I swallow what feels like a fur ball and answer before it's too late.

"Sure," I say, feeling everything except what that word implies. I want to look at Ranan, but each time I do my courage deflates like a leaky balloon. So, I don't look at him. Instead, I stare at Sempuku with my best version of "cool" slapped on my face.

"Good," he says, with a grin that tells me I've walked straight into something, but it's way too late. "Ranan will tell you where you can find one. You must catch it and bring it to me. Alive."

They're laughing again and I know I would be, too, if it wasn't me who's about to find out the difference between a huntsman and the Kenyan variety of oversized arachnid. But then, they seem to spend so much time magnifying their own egos. Maybe their spiders aren't that big at all. This is my one consolation in what's turning into a downpour of doubt.

I look at Ranan, but he's looking at the ground – like he's picking out the best spot to dig my grave.

∿∿∿∿∿

My skin's crawling and it's like a giant itch that you just can't scratch.

Ranan's been gone for five minutes now, off with the cows, and it's hot beneath the acacias, but at least there are no baboons in sight. In my backpack, there's a pair of gloves, which I guess is kind of cheating, but I forgot to ask if the spider is venomous and the nearest hospital, as far as I know, is back in Nairobi. I've also got a camping pot, which I'm going to use as a trap.

I didn't tell Dad because there's something about a spider's hairy legs and the way they creep around that just freaks him out, which is probably not the best thing to be filling my head with right now.

I'm squatting next to a burrow by the root of an acacia and there's a web covering the mouth of it, which says keep out to me. But I can't.

Sempuku's victorious grin is hanging there in my memory, and I need to wipe it out. I get a stick – the longest one I can find – and pull out the pot. Suddenly, I start to laugh to myself, which I've heard is the first sign of madness.

At least there's no audience. This is the first time I've done anything since we got to Enkasara without someone or something looking on. I look round once more to make sure I'm really alone.

I pull at the web with the stick and hear a hiss. My mind's making jigsaws of a strange African animal, half snake, half spider, and I wish I could just jump on the Internet and check all this out. Except, right now, there's just me, my stick, the pot and a bitter taste in my mouth.

I poke the stick into the hole and something grabs hold of it. It's strong and I want to take a look, but my body pulls back – it's telling me that this is more than I bargained for. Whatever's in that hole has latched on, so I make like a fisherman and haul it out.

Hanging off the end of the stick, with fangs like crab claws, is the biggest spider I've ever imagined, let alone seen. It's the size of my dad's hand, with his fingers spread, and it's brown and hairy and ferocious. It's out of my league.

The spider drops off the stick and heads back into its burrow. I'm just letting the air fill my lungs again when I nearly choke on it. The spider has darted out again, and it's more than mad. I leap back, landing in the dust, but it's gone once more, and all I can hear is its hissing and the bongos in my heart.

Suddenly, I can't quite remember what I'm doing here and all I want is to go back to the village and have a nice cup of milky tea. Maybe help Dad clean his cameras again, or even write an essay on life in a Maasai village to send to my class. But I can't, because this is one of those moments, one of the few in your life, and it's not just about wiping the smart look off an annoying *moran*'s face. This is all about me.

So I pick up my stick and I move towards the gaping hole. I decide that first I need a plan, and gradually it comes to me – I'm no super-brain but I've got more neurons than a spider and I still have size on my side.

First of all, I dig a hole close to the burrow with my hands. The continued hissing turns my arms to jelly. I keep my eyes tuned for movement because, every now and then, the spider pops out, its legs raised like spears and full of aggression. I know that he'll bite. I'm resisting the urge to flee, but it's sending me into a sweat.

I twist the pot into the hole I've made and pick up my stick. This is it and I look up at the sky, searching for something to give me a blessing, but there's only a bird with long tail feathers that seems more interested in itself.

I plunge the stick into the hole. The spider's got hold of it again and it's pulling, like it wants to drag me in there and eat me alive. I yank the stick with all of my might and haul the spider out of its lair, feeling the weight of it suspended on the end of the stick. I realise that, if it leaps, or flicks its body, it could land right on my legs. Then I hear a snap. It's bitten right through the stick. With a clunk way too loud for an insect, it falls into the pot.

I grab the pot lid and slam it down, but the spider's so strong it's banging on it, trying to push it off. I jump up and slam my foot down to hold the lid in place. The tapping of those powerful legs against the lid is terrifying. The hairs on the back of my neck shoot up, sending a chain reaction through my body, making me feel sure that I'm going to throw up.

I don't, though. I undo my belt and wrap it around the pot, fastening it tight. And then I just sit there and catch my breath, half expecting the birds to land on my shoulders and whisper praise in my ear.

fourteen

I think the spider's asleep.

It stopped making noise a while ago and all I can think about is, what if it's dead and I have to do this all over again. I chuck a stone at the pot and the tinny sound is followed by a hissing. It's alive.

This is turning into the longest afternoon of my life. I'm torn between wanting to get the whole thing over and done with or drawing out the time between then and now. It's nice here, under the trees, just me and my bloodthirsty spider.

Except there's another noise. I recognise it straight away – it's Ranan coming with the cattle to take me back to the village. I'm happy, because I'm not doing this without my friend.

"Ash, you there?"

I pick up the pot, check the belt's still fastened tight, and move out from under the shade of the trees. Ranan's standing there, leaning on his stick, glad to see me with my arms, legs and fingers still attached.

"You have a spider?" he asks, eyes darting.

"In here," I say, dangling the pot in front of him. Ranan steps backwards, his jaw landing on his chest.

"Really? You caught a giant spider?"

I now realise that he hadn't really expected me to succeed.

"Of course." I frown. "No big deal. I'm not afraid of spiders." The hissing starts up again and the spider moves so violently I drop the pot on the ground.

Ranan's already behind a tree, so he doesn't see me nearly swallow my tonsils as I leap back and land on my backside. I get up quickly, grab hold of the pot and shove it in my pack.

"Come on, Ranan. Time to get back."

Ranan comes out from behind the tree. "I don't like spiders. They are …" His face screws up in disgust.

"Ugly …. hairy … creepy?" I say. It just makes him cringe more. "Don't worry. When we get to the village, I'll handle everything – you just stick close to me."

As I say this I feel braver. What have I got to worry about, I've already done battle with the giant and come out on top. Besides, from what I can see, the Maasai seem to be terrified of huge hairy spiders, making them part of a very large club.

Ranan's quiet all the way back, so I just concentrate on what I'm going to say to earn the most bravery points. All it's going to need is the truth, minus a few unnecessary, nearly-dissolving-with-fright details.

As soon as we get close to Enkasara, kids start running out to meet us – word's got around. Then Sempuku and the *moran* come over.

Sempuku walks straight up to me, with his row of mates behind him, and he has a smile on his face.

"So, Ashani, the famous spider warrior. Did you complete your task?"

The *moran* all crack up, as the children form

a circle around us, not wanting to miss a word. I have my audience and this is my moment. I take a deep breath. "I did."

Suddenly, I have their attention. Sempuku turns back to the others and they're whispering among themselves. Ranan steps up behind me and I can sense that he's there, so I whisper to him, "Stay with me, Ranan. Whatever happens, stay with me."

Sempuku is grinning. They obviously don't believe me.

"Okay, now you must show us," he says, and more snickers go round.

As I take off my backpack and place it on the ground, the kids step back, making the circle bigger, and a hush goes through the crowd. I can feel their fear and it's taking away my own. I'm in charge here, which gives me power, something I can do with right now. Ranan holds his ground as I told him to. It feels good to have him with me as I pull the pot out. A hiss fills the air.

I catch a terrified glint in Sempuku's eye and it's enough to fire me up. They know I've done it. I've passed my initiation, but something inside me wants more. I need a spectacular victory and, as the buzzing rises in my head, I take hold of my belt buckle on the pot and begin to slip the leather through.

The circle widens further and the hush is now a gasp, mixed with hissing, and the tink-tink of the spider thrashing to get out. Then the lid is off and the spider leaps to the ground, sending everyone into a panic. Kids scream and run away, while Ranan and I stand still.

My guts have gone liquid, but my legs are like rock. I hold my stick in front of me and prepare for a fight. Then, my eyes are drawn to Sempuku and the *moran*, who are slowly stepping back, hands out in front of them, their clubs raised. A secret smile creeps up on my face, and it seems I'm not the only one that's noticed them – the spider has scuttled round to their side of the circle and it's rearing up at them.

The *moran* freeze and for a moment I'm sure they're going to club my prize into a furry lump, when the spider runs towards them. Somebody lets out a scream. I hope it's Sempuku, but in the confusion I never find out, because they're backing away quickly, then fleeing – with the spider in pursuit.

I turn round to Ranan who is making like a stunned monkey. I can see that his body is still with me, but his mind is half way up the nearest tree. Then a grin explodes all over my face.

"Ash, you okay?"

I'm so okay I'm laughing, every part of me shaking. This is a feeling I want to hang on to for the rest of my life. I put my hand on his shoulder and say, "Hey, thanks for sticking with me."

"No problem," he says with a slow smile, but I can see it wasn't easy. Then it's his turn to take me by surprise. "Now I know the true Ashani."

Stuff's whirling round inside me and it's not just about proving a point. Right now, it's like the world just came together and decided to sing me a song, and the words are all about how great it is to be alive.

fifteen

Turns out the spider isn't poisonous – not unless you're allergic – but they really like to bite.

Tell me something I don't know. I reckon I'm lucky I still have ten fingers, because that spider could perform an amputation with its eyes closed and all eight legs tied behind its back.

It's called a king baboon and it's a type of tarantula – I found it in Dad's scary African insect book.

Since the spider episode, I have a fan club twice as big as the one I used to have just because I'm white. Kids keep popping up all over the place, wanting to hold my hand. Whenever I'm in the village, they stick to me like flies with superglue for shoes.

Even the *moran* looked at me differently –

like I was only half loser.

The *moran* hung around for a couple of days and then they were off again, giving sideways glances at the bushes as they went, making sure that tarantula was nowhere in sight.

Today, Ranan and I are going on our own sort of walkabout. He's taking me to the village where he used to go to school. It's hot and dusty, as usual, and it's taking longer than a week of maths tests to get there.

I can't imagine walking that far every day just to go to school, but the Maasai don't seem to mind.

The village is almost identical to Enkasara, except for the school, which is really just a big open hut with benches.

"It is closed for the holidays. The teacher goes back home," Ranan says, showing me around.

It's empty, except for a couple of little kids playing in the dirt under the benches with a truck made out of old pineapple jam cans.

"So, where are the desks?"

"What is desk?"

"You know, tables to write on," I explain.

"We write on paper."

Sometimes it's hard trying to explain what it's like living in a different world.

"Your school is the same?"

"Not exactly. There's more stuff, but the same idea," I say, trying to imagine kids from my class sitting on those dusty benches, making stuff out of old cans. "So, what does your teacher do when kids muck around?"

"Muck around? What is this?"

"Don't listen, play games when the teacher's talking, stuff like that."

Ranan looks at me like I've just led one of his cows over the edge of a cliff. And I know it's one of those moments when things fall into the space between our different cultures. Ranan says, "We respect our teacher very much. It is an honour to go to school. Nobody makes trouble."

No wonder Miss Rawlings loves Africa – this is a teacher's paradise. All I say is, "School's great," because he looks like he's about to disown meand I'll have to navigate my own way home.

Ranan smiles. "Good. Come, I'll show you."

At the other side of the village, near a road, are some rickety old huts. He points to them proudly and says, "Shops."

They look like one puff of wind would fold them up like a house of cards, but inside they're packed full of things, stacked up on dusty wooden shelves. A regular Maasai shopping mall.

"Hey, Ranan, want a drink?"

"Yes. Please."

I walk over to the closest hut. The old guy inside must have heard me coming, because he wakes up. He looks surprised to see me – maybe he thinks he's still dreaming. I guess they don't get too many white kids dropping in for takeaways this time of year.

"Two Cokes, please."

The old man bends down and grabs two bottles from under the counter. I wonder what else he's got under there, but I figure peanut butter might be pushing my luck. I pay the guy and walk back over to Ranan.

"Sorry, they're warm."

Ranan smiles and doesn't seem to care. I guess that's what comes from growing up without a fridge. We sit in the shade of the hut and sip our drinks slowly. They're better than Christmas after so many cups of milky Maasai tea.

We watch the few people who go by and try to keep the flies from dive-bombing our drinks. I don't think words like "hurry" and "timetable" would feature in a Maa dictionary. Sometimes Ranan and I don't say or do anything for such a long time that we could be auditioning as mannequins for a window display.

I still have a little change left in my pocket, so I decide to buy some tomatoes and a few bananas for Ranan's mum. I know how pleased she'll be and I reckon it's a good idea to keep whoever's cooking your meals on side.

When I return, Ranan's still sitting in the shade dealing with a boomerang fly that just keeps coming back. He looks up at me and says, "It is time to go."

"Yeah, before we get eaten alive."

The sun is starting to go down, but it's still warm and Enkasara seems a long way off. It's like our legs are made of punching bags and we have chewing gum stuck to the bottom of our feet.

∿∿∿∿∿

"Look," Ranan whispers.

I look around to see him pointing at a soft patch of ground. In the dust, there are all kinds of footprints and animal tracks and I can even make out the pattern of my new walking boots where I must have trodden when I was trying to catch him up.

"So, we've been going round in circles. Big deal."

"No, look!"

I look, then I see. "Wow!"

Right next to my boot print is one great big paw print that doesn't belong to the kind of cat that hangs around Gran's garden waiting for birds to drop out of the trees. The tracks lead off in the direction of the village where we've just been. I wonder how long it's been since the lion passed by this way in search of a meal. Ranan bends down to show me something else.

"First Ashani, then the lion."

I bend down next to him to take a closer look. The lion's print overlaps the mark left by my boots, which can only mean one thing. I look round to make sure we're alone – we passed by here only minutes ago, so that lion could be anywhere. Suddenly, every bush and every rustle seems ready to pounce on us and treat us like afternoon tea.

My first reflex is to run, to get as much distance between us and these prints as I can. I imagine the lion watching us, listening to my thoughts – a drooling grin curling up his face.

"Do you think he can smell us?" I say, because I can smell everything now the adrenalin has kicked in. I wonder if the lion can sense it in me as it prepares to spring.

"We must return quickly to Enkasara."

"You don't need to be a warrior to work that one out," I say, a snort sneaking out like a valve letting off pressure.

Ranan's not impressed. "It is not funny."

"Who's laughing?" I say, but I can see his mind's going in another direction.

"If something happens to you, there is much trouble."

"Yeah, my dad wouldn't be too thrilled," I say, looking around, not wanting to cut him off, but needing to get home.

His head is jerking around, keeping an eye on the terrain, but also trying to shake something loose. "Big trouble if a white man is killed."

"So, you don't care about me? You're just worried about getting your village in trouble? That's what it's all about, isn't it, always the village first. What about me, Ranan, and what about you? Don't we count for something on our own?"

"Yes. As part of the group."

For a second, thoughts of lions are replaced by thoughts I never knew were there. I'm thinking these people are stupid, they don't understand – that Ranan's just a kid who's kidding himself he's warrior material.

A thousand words shoot into my mouth and I want to let them go, let them hit their target, but Ranan's face stops me in the nick of time. It shows two messages clear as day upon it – one says, apprentice warrior working on his fear; the other, it's good to belong.

Ranan heads off in the direction of Enkasara. I follow his dark back. He's so sure of what he's part of and I know that, even if the lion is still out there, ready to attack, I won't be alone.

sixteen

Ranan hasn't said a single word all the way home, which is making me feel about as safe as a packet of chocolate biscuits in a room full of chocoholics, but I can see the smoke rising and I know Enkasara is not far off.

As we come through familiar trees, Ranan heads straight to his hut and seems glad to find Moses at home. They talk quietly together for a while and, although I've got a hundred things to say, I don't want to interrupt, so I just wait outside.

Then Dad turns up. "Hey, Ash, you all right? Looks like you just saw a ghost."

"Worse. We just saw lion's tracks – its footprint was on top of mine."

Dad looks like he's about to introduce me to what he had for lunch. Ranan and Moses come out.

"Moses. Ranan and Ash have just seen a lion's tracks and it looks like it walked right over where they'd been. It might even have followed them here."

Dad is now looking the way I felt up until about ten minutes ago, but all of a sudden I'm coming over brave. I've experienced something he hasn't and I like the way that feels.

"We're back now and we're fine."

"Hmmm. I guess I knew there could be lions around, but it didn't seem real. Not until now."

His face is full of uncertainty and I can see he's wrestling with ideas that won't stand in line. Moses puts his hand on Dad's shoulder.

"It is not unusual to see lion tracks. There is no reason to worry."

But the way Ranan's avoiding my eyes makes me wonder if Moses is telling the whole truth. I have a feeling that it has something to do with the lion being on his own. Maybe that's not good.

But then, as Gran's always saying, I do have a hyperactive imagination.

"No reason to worry," I repeat, giving Dad one of my most cool-calm-and-collected smiles. "Moses is right. Besides, how many guys can say a lion has walked in their footsteps?"

Dad laughs, but there's a chance the whole thing's going under and I'll end up grounded in the village, slapping cow dung on cracks in the wall. So I dive in to save the situation.

"Anyway, Ranan was there to look after me the whole time."

Suddenly, something sinks in. Ever since I got here, Ranan has stuck close, followed me round like a mother warthog, nose to the wind. He's always ready to explain, teach and guide me. I've never been alone, except yesterday with the spider, although something tells me, in some way, he was hanging round even then. Lurking behind the acacias, in case something went wrong.

Part of me wants to shout, "Hey, I can do this on my own," but another, truer part of me keeps repeating the message I read on Ranan's face – it's good to belong.

Dad cuts in. "Yeah, well, safety in numbers and all that, but I'd rather you stick around here tomorrow all the same."

"Sure, Dad," I say, thinking I can give him a day to get over nearly losing his one and only kid. But then I'll be out there again with my new freedom, the one that comes from being trusted and knowing you're part of a team.

"What do you think Gran would make of all of this?" he asks and I wonder if he wouldn't prefer someone else to make the decisions for him, especially when it counts.

"I think she would be proud of us," I say, and suddenly I want to write her a letter and tell her everything that's happened – including the scary stuff, the whole lot. Let her know that I'm changing, for the good, and that I'm learning the kind of stuff you need to know to become a man.

The only problem is that, once I've written it, the nearest postbox is in the village, back the way we came, along the track marked with boot, sandal and lion paw prints.

Dad's typing in the shade of Moses' hut when I get back from a walk around the *enkang*.

He's sitting on an old stool, wearing only a piece of material around his waist. His laptop is balanced on a plank that's resting on a couple of empty tins. Above him, Ranan's mum is putting a fresh layer of dung on the roof of the hut, and I'm thinking how glad I am that the kids don't get stuck with that job – mud pies is one thing, but dung pancakes, no way. Funny thing is, she seems to be enjoying herself.

"Do you have any idea how feral you look?" I say to Dad, rubbing my forehead because I've got a bit of a headache.

"What? Haven't you ever seen a guy dressed like this using a laptop out the front of his mud hut before?"

"Now you mention it … no."

With the laptop connected to a solar panel, he looks like a high-tech version of Tarzan.

"Well, you live and learn," he says, closing his laptop. "You all right, Ash? You look a bit ill."

"I'm just feeling a bit tired. Ranan kept pushing me off the mattress in the middle of the night."

"All part of living in a Maasai village," he

says, flicking a fly off his arm. "Hey, Henry is picking us up in a week It's kind of weird to think we'll be leaving soon, don't you think?"

"Yeah, I've got used to living here."

Standing there with Ranan's mum looking down at us, her hands all covered in dung, it's almost impossible to imagine being back in Australia, living my old life – going to school!

"Hello, Daniel. Ashani."

"Hey, Moses. No sign of the lion?"

Moses smiles. "I will be sure to tell you if he comes visiting. I am here to talk of a celebration – it is to honour your visit, because you will soon be leaving."

"A party. Unreal!"

Dad looks mega-pleased – having a party thrown for you by a bunch of Maasai is definitely better than a poke in the eye with a blunt spear. "Then, Moses, you must let us buy a goat to help in the celebrations."

"How's a goat going to help – do a song and dance routine?" I joke. Dad laughs, whether out of loyalty or embarrassment, it's hard to tell.

"The people will be very happy," says Moses, glad that Ranan is his son, instead of me.

Everybody in a Maasai village likes a good party because they get to eat meat, and goat isn't as bad as it sounds. It's a million times better than that *ugali* they usually eat, which tastes like a cross between porridge and the glue Gran used when she wallpapered her bedroom. And, if I ever have to eat another *chapatti*, I think I'll puke so hard I'll have to pick my intestines out of my teeth. I read in a book that the Maasai drink cows' blood mixed with milk, but so far nobody's offered me anything like that, and I certainly haven't been begging for a taste.

Once or twice since I got here I have even fantasised about brussels sprouts – not because I'm starving or anything, but they'd make a nice change. You could write every Maasai recipe I've come across on the nail of your big toe and still have room left over for illustrations.

But at least nobody goes hungry. Dad says it's because the rains have been good. When there's a drought heaps of cattle die and food gets expensive. Then even a bowl of *ugali* would seem like Christmas dinner at my gran's.

When he told me that, I felt weird. I tried to

imagine Ranan looking like the people you see on TV with stomachs like sheep that have died and bloated in the heat. On TV it doesn't look real. But Ranan's more than just real – he's my mate.

"Moses, what happens here when there's a drought?"

He gives me a kind of where-did-that-come-from look and then he says quietly, "It is difficult, but we survive. We have always survived."

I suddenly feel like I'm going to faint and I'm wondering whether it's the *mandazi* we shared with the flies for breakfast, except my stomach feels okay.

"Are you all right, Ash?" asks Dad, as I lean against him, the *enkang* going into a spin.

"Not really."

Dad puts his hand on my forehead. "You're pretty hot. You'd better go lie down."

"Yeah, good idea," I say, flopping in his arms.

By the time he's got me rolled up in my sleeping bag, I'm shaking like a palm in the wind and dreaming of my bed back home.

Adventures aren't much fun when you're feeling sick.

Ranan's mother, Nataiya, comes in with a bowl of water and a cloth and starts wiping down my forehead, while Moses and Dad whisper by the door. I know it's them because I recognise their voices, even though their bodies are just big blobs against a very loud sky.

Their words are starting to chase each other loosely round my head and I try to hang on to them, line them up in rows that make sense. But I can't. Except I manage to grab hold of one word, one I'd like to throw back.

The word is "malaria", and it's mixed in with a sound like running water from a half-open tap. I could do with a drink right now, but, when I go to ask for one, nothing comes out. Because the words get caught up and strangled by the realisation that I'm going to die.

seventeen

The ceiling is made of flies. Layer upon swarming layer of them. Their mirrored wings catch tiny specks of light and reflect it into my eyes.

My bed is crawling. Things are weaving their way through the branches my bed is made of. A baboon's hand grabs at my sleeping bag, the long hissing hairy legs of a giant spider poke into my back and roll me over, winding me up in a sticky web of strange thoughts.

Smiling Nataiya floats in, smelling of sweet milk and dung and the smoke of the fire that never goes out. She raises her hand to me and I feel water soaking into my hair, mingling with sweat, running saltiness between my dry lips.

She speaks to me, but I hear only buzzing, then a song. I'm not sure if she's singing it, or it's coming from somewhere else. It's my mother, holding out her hand, her long hair brushing my hot cheek as my face melts – water, sweat, tears. I hear her inside my head. She's whispering. "Ashani," she says, "my little one, you are not alone."

Dad enters the hut and he feels solid, like a big rolling ball of strength, making its way towards me, settling next to my bed. His hand feels sturdy on my forehead, but his eyes are filled with fear.

I hear him whisper, "What have I done?" And I'm wondering what it is he's done wrong, when a tear falls on my cheek. And I want to speak, to say I'm okay, but I'm pinned to the bed under a layer of invisible concrete, and I ask myself, am I dead?

Then he's gone and I'm asleep, or I think I am, I'm not sure, because on the wall of the hut I see my dream. The one with the lion and me and the darkness. In my hand, there's the spear. I clench my fist around its solidness and stare at my enemy, his eyes locked on me, his roar in my ears, but my spear isn't shrinking this time.

The room wobbles and for a moment I think I've woken up and that my dream has disappeared, that the flies are coming for me. Then my dream floats back into focus. As I stare at the two of us – the lion and the boy – I step into the kid clinging to the spear and realise that, standing next to me, shoulder to shoulder, is somebody else.

Nataiya's sitting over me when I come to.

"Daniel," she calls, and instantly my dad is at the door.

"Ash – thank God." Relief is visible all over his body.

"Dad, how long … ?"

He's bending down to help me up on to my elbows. "You've been out for twenty-four hours. You had me worried there for a while."

"Malaria?" I ask, still a bit short on words.

"The real thing."

"But I thought we couldn't catch it."

Dad is smiling as he hands me some water. "The pills we have been taking are a form of treatment. They don't stop you getting malaria, they just help you fight it if you do. I had to give you some stronger medicine, otherwise …"

He drops his eyes to the ground and I can see he's had a hard time of it.

"I'm okay now, Dad," I say, trying to get out of bed.

"Save your strength. We've got the celebration tomorrow night. You need to rest for that."

"Dad, can I ask you something?"

"Sure, what is it?"

"When I was sick, I saw some weird things."

"You were hallucinating – you were calling out and some of it was pretty strange."

My brain is still foggy, but one image remains very clear. "I saw Mum."

"What did you see?" asks Dad, sitting down beside me.

"It's to do with that lion dream I had when I was little. I kept seeing that while I was sick. But one time was more like a memory, and I'm wondering if it's true."

"Go on," Dad says, looking interested.

"I'm with Mum. I'm looking up at her and I'm holding her hand. She's wearing a blue dress."

Dad smiles. "I know the dress you're talking

about. It was her favourite."

"And I think we're at the zoo, because I know there are animals around and lots of people, and suddenly I feel sick, like I'm going to throw up, because all I can hear is the roar of a lion. And Mum's looking at me and she's afraid."

Dad's sitting quietly, staring at the dirt floor, and I want to know what he's thinking, but I let him take his time.

"We went to the zoo not long before your mum died, Ash, but I don't remember anything about a lion."

"In my memory, you aren't there."

"Maybe I went to buy ice-cream," he says, but his mind's on something else. "Ash, do you think in your mind you connected the lion's roar with your mum dying and that's why you had those dreams?"

"I don't know, Dad," I say. Things are starting to go into a spin again. "I think I need to rest."

"Sure, Ash. Take all the time you need."

There are so many thoughts all mixed up, sucking up my energy, that I dissolve into my sleeping bag and am absorbed into sleep.

eighteen

The night of the party, the village looks like a Christmas parade with an African theme.

Everybody's dressed up, wearing truckloads of jewellery, so I put on all the pieces I've been given. I hang huge earrings over my ears, which makes everyone laugh, but I'm not about to pierce them with a baseball bat.

Ranan's even convinced me to dress up like a Maasai. Dad's cracking up about the whole thing when Moses comes in carrying a bright red sheet for Dad and his very own pair of recycled-tyre sandals. In the old days, they used to make them out of leather, but you get a whole lot more mileage out of a pair of retreads than a cow's rear end.

"Hey, Dad. Just think of how useful they'd be on a motorbike. You could use them to slow down if your brakes weren't working."

"Yeah. But, boy, do they stink!"

Dad's got really hairy legs and he usually wears trousers, so they're whiter than an albino polar bear, and furrier, too. Not a good look sticking out from under a red sheet.

"Check your arms out," I say, because they're tanned only halfway up as he's always dressed in a T-shirt or a shirt with the sleeves rolled up.

"Quit laughing and chuck us over a couple of those bracelets."

He puts some bright, beaded bracelets over the spot where the white turns to brown, which looks even worse, but then my dad's never had much fashion sense.

"Gran would kill herself laughing if she could see you now. Well, she will actually, as soon as I show her the photos."

Dad makes a grab for the camera, but he's too slow and I'm already dreaming about the new mountain bike I'll get in exchange for the photos of Dad dressed up like this.

Nataiya comes in and I feel silly all of a sudden. She's carrying a bowl of red ochre, which she offers to us and places on the floor in front of Dad. With red ochre on our bodies, we look a bit better – more convincing.

Ranan is watching as we get ready, so I ask him, "Aren't you going to get dressed up, too?"

"I am not yet a warrior. It is not right."

I'm thinking about whether it's right for me to be doing all this stuff when he says, "It is time to start the celebrations."

We head out. A group of elders stand around talking about something that seems important and I'm wondering what they're getting so serious about while we're having a party. Ranan explains. "They have chosen new names for you and Daniel. Your Maasai names."

"But I like my name – I admit it gets me in a lot of fights at school, but I'm used to that."

Besides, I'm kind of proud of it. Mum and Dad chose it together when they were travelling and named me after some cool Himalayan monk.

"Ashani is a good name. We want to give you Maasai name as well. It is a gift."

Most of the Maasai I have met have an English name from school as well as a Maasai name, and one or two nicknames thrown in on top of those. Still, choosing new names can't be easy, because a couple of the old guys are starting to get a bit annoyed. It would be funny, except everyone respects the elders, and laughing at them is like poking fun at Jedi knights.

Suddenly, the talking stops and they all look pleased with themselves. I lean over and whisper to Dad, "I hope they've chosen cool names for us because some of the people in the *enkang* have some pretty strange ones."

"Yeah. What about that guy Nolkipenperia? What a mouthful."

"I tried calling him 'the incredible Nolk', but nobody else seems to get the joke."

Dad looks at me like he wants me to give him a break and then turns back to face the elders.

"*Embuku,*" says one of the elders to my dad.

"*Embuku,*" Dad repeats, trying to get his tongue round his new name.

Moses is explaining to Dad what he should do. As the elders come over one by one and repeat Dad's new name, he has to say "*eeo*".

"*Embuku.*"

"*Eeo.*"

Then it's my turn.

"*Motonyi.*"

"*Eeo.*"

Motonyi. I have heard that word before. "Hey, Ranan, what does *motonyi* mean?"

"Bird."

"Why bird?"

"They say you are like a little bird with white feathers. Always talking and soon you will fly away."

I was kind of hoping for something a little more brave or powerful, but then again, "bird" is better than "mangy warthog", or "pond slime", so I can't really complain.

"What about *Embuku*?"

"It is from the Maasai word for book. Daniel reads many books and writes many things on his laptop."

Laptop. Dad taught him that word, although it's not all that useful in a Maasai village. "Flies" would have to go on top of any list of essential words. But then maybe one day Ranan will live somewhere else. He may get a job in Nairobi and use a laptop and think of us. Somehow, though, I just can't imagine him in jeans and a T-shirt, or a suit, walking around a big city on his own. I can only see him surrounded by his family, his village and his *moran* friends.

After the naming ceremony is over, everybody starts getting stuck into the food. Dad bought a lot for the celebration, including some soft drinks for the kids. It's our way of saying thank you, and everybody is looking as happy as a monkey in a bathful of bananas.

The goat has been cut into small pieces and roasted on long sticks. It's being passed around for everyone to have a bit. The elders are sitting in a group, drinking something that seems to be good, judging by the way they're gulping it down.

"What's that?"

Ranan smiles and takes another sip of his lemonade. "They drink honey beer. It is good for laughing."

Apart from the mud huts and the other small details, it's funny how some things are the same all over. Here I am, smack-bang in the middle of Maasailand, having a barbecue with beer in a backyard full of flies. And the only thing that's missing is a party-size bottle of tomato sauce.

~~~~~~~~

That honey beer must be good stuff.

When Ranan and I get up to have a pee at dawn, some of the old guys are still carrying on, singing like a group of vervet monkeys that have been eating overripe fruit.

I take a good look around me – we'll soon be on our way and Enkasara will be just a bunch of memories. Ranan is finished and he's standing quietly watching the sky change colour, pulling his blanket up around his shoulders because it's cold enough to make a flamingo turn blue. It seems the right moment, so I ask him, "Are you afraid?"

He gives me a curious look, but he knows what I'm talking about. I wonder if he's about to give me the old "We Maasai are never afraid" routine, when he says, "I am not afraid to become a warrior. I am only afraid I won't make my family proud."

I can't imagine Moses being anything but proud of his son. I wonder if people think the same thing when they look at me and Dad.

"You already make your family proud and

I'm proud to be your friend."

I've never been very good at telling people how I feel about them, but the look on his face tells me I should give it a go more often.

"Me also."

I decide to try him on another biggie. "I know it probably sounds a bit of a stupid question, but … what does it really mean to be a warrior?"

Ranan pulls his *shuka* further up on to his shoulders and stares at the trees. "It's not something to know with the head. It's …" He searches for the right words. "It is something that you feel. Inside."

He taps himself on his chest with his flat hand and turns to look at me, which spurs me on. "And how do you know if you are ready?"

"You will know."

I am about to say, "I was talking about you, not me," when I realise it's all the same thing. At least to him and, now, maybe to me also. I remember something Henry said about all men having a warrior inside of them. As I stare into Ranan's eyes, just as the Maasai do, I say with certainty, "I will know."

He nods and takes one last look at the

changing sky before going back towards the hut. Wrapped up in his *shuka*, walking silently towards the rising sun he seems a lot older and wiser than the kid I first met.

In fact, everything seems different. It's like I went to sleep and woke up in some movie, where all the heroes are my friends.

nineteen

To celebrate our last day in the village, Ranan has organised some time off for us to go hunting – just birds and other small game.

"It is part of our preparation to be warriors," says Ranan, slipping on his retreads.

"Like hunting a lion?"

"Yes," he says.

I wonder how he feels about lion hunting being illegal these days. I realise the biggest regret I have about leaving, apart from, well, so many things, is that I haven't had a full-on experience with a lion.

I start going through my list of "almosts" – in Odinga's shop I smelled a lion for the first time; we saw the real thing in the national park, but from inside a car; near the village I even saw a lion's tracks. But still I wonder what it would be like coming face to face with a lion, with just a spear in my hand.

"Hey, Ranan. What would you do if you saw a lion when you were out with the cattle?"

"I have seen a lion."

Now he really has my attention. "Really? What did you do?"

"He was far away. He wasn't hungry. I moved the cattle to a safe place."

"What would you do if one tried to kill a cow, or even you?"

Ranan looks at me like I'm stupid. "I would fight."

I know he would rather die than do something that would make his family look bad, but me, I'm not so sure. Maybe I'd be up the first tree faster than you can say, "That lion's got teeth bigger than a baobab tree." I mean, spiders are one thing, but lions, well, it's healthy to be afraid of them – it might just keep you alive.

We head off in a different direction to where we normally take the herd, straight into a clump of acacias. Ranan shows me where the boys keep their spears hidden in the hollow of a tree. They aren't the real thing like the *moran* have – the ones with long metal spikes on their ends. The boys' spears are only made of wood that's been sharpened to a point, but they look like they'll do the trick anyway.

We keep walking until the trees get thicker, becoming almost a forest. "Here, there are many animals," says Ranan, looking totally cool holding his spear.

I wonder whether I look as good as he does? I'm wearing Maasai jewellery and I've got my own spear, but I have trousers and my walking boots on.

We move along quietly, not talking much because we have to listen for animals. I've been stalking animals in the bush before at home, but we used torches not spears. I know some kids who go hunting with their dads, but that's different, because they take guns and the animals don't have a chance.

We stop for a while and Ranan shows me how to hold the spear. We practise throwing it at a target he's made out of some dried grass and hung in a tree. After a couple of goes, I stop missing the tree completely and once I almost get it in the centre of the target. Okay, so it's not a moving target, but it's my first day on the job.

"We are ready," Ranan says, with a big smile on his face. He looks keen to take on a whole tribe of baboons single-handed, wearing a blindfold and balancing on one foot.

We walk slowly with our spears high above our heads, keeping our eyes peeled for anything that moves. I spot a whydah bird with really long tail feathers and nod my head at Ranan to show him where it is. We move closer, like a couple of Apaches on the warpath – or two Maasai warriors on a hunt.

I hold my breath because even that seems loud, but it just makes my heart beat twice as fast. It's so noisy I might as well use a microphone and speakers and shout, "Look out, we're armed!"

Suddenly, behind us, the trees begin to move – something is stampeding towards us through the forest. Ranan's eyes are wide open, his spear ready to meet the threat, while I hold mine above my head so tightly my arm's shaking like an electric toothbrush that has gone into overdrive.

Crashing through the trees, they come at a fast pace.

It's a group of *moran* and they're well armed. Their bodies are all shiny, like they've been rolling round in bathtubs full of margarine. Their legs are covered in red ochre stripes. Around their ankles they have tied some cowbells that they've stuffed with grass. Something's up.

They surround us and all begin to talk at once. They're explaining something to Ranan in Maa when I see that one of them is Sempuku and go over to talk to him. "What's going on?"

"We are hunting for a lion," he says, shaking so much with excitement that he looks like he's just eaten his own weight in chocolate.

"But I thought you weren't allowed."

"This lion killed a child in a village near here, so now we must kill it. For this it is allowed."

All I can think about is the lion whose tracks we saw, and whether it was the same one, when Ranan comes over to me and puts his hand on my shoulder. "Are you ready?"

At that exact moment, I realise that it's for real. Today we will go hunting – not for small birds, but for a king. I wonder what Dad would think, but he isn't here, and this time it's up to me – it's up to us.

"I'm ready," I say, before any second thoughts have time to take hold of my brain. This is the moment I've been waiting for and I'm not going to let a serious case of "I'm too young to die" get in the way of things, even if my guts are in my socks.

Ranan looks at Sempuku, as if asking for his permission, then a look goes round the group and I realise the whole thing could be over for me before it has even started. They speak quietly between themselves, their heads leaning in, forming a circle, and then suddenly they stop. They turn to face Ranan and me. I'm about to pass out from the suspense when Sempuku gives a nod. A *moran* moves forward and hands me a spear, a real one, while another hands Ranan a club.

Then everyone's on the move, running swiftly through the forest, Ranan and I right at the back with the guy who gave me the spear.

From time to time, we slow down as they check for signs that the lion has passed this way. By the looks on their faces, and the way they grip their spears, I know we are hot on its trail.

And they're chanting "*eele, eele*" like they are calling to it, summoning it to its death, and the singing's getting into my head, working its way through my blood, and I find myself joining in – "*eele, eele*", the words slipping off my tongue like they've always been there just waiting to get out.

Once or twice I pinch myself just to make sure I'm not having some weird kind of flashback to a past life when I was cool. The funny thing is that I don't feel afraid. It's more like a case of hyperactive butterflies that keep bouncing off the walls of my stomach. I look down, but I can't see anything, not even my heart doing double back flips, and I nearly bump into Ranan as the *moran* slow down, then stop.

"He is very near," Ranan says. He's shaking, too. His skin's all shiny and he looks like the warrior he's about to become.

The group start moving again, but really

slowly, and so quietly I'm afraid that each time I take a step, my big boots will give us away. I wish I was wearing sandals like them, even if they hurt your feet and make them stink.

Suddenly, I hear a roar behind me – not like in the movies, because even the best surround-sound couldn't come close. The whole forest shakes and I'm sure that at any second the leaves will curl up and drop off with fright.

I spin around. The guy who gave me the spear is on the ground, arms thrown back, shield dropped, face squashed up with fear. A lion is pinning him down.

I freeze. I'm the closest. It takes a split second for the others to turn around and maybe another before they move into place. It seems like forever. Like a slow-motion replay on TV. The only thing I can hear is breathing – my own breath like a bull in my ear.

The lion looks straight into my eyes. It's a male and his dark eyes are surrounded by a huge mane. He fixes his stare on me. Half terrified, half ready to kill – just like me.

Then everything speeds up again – the frozen moment broken. The *moran* move quickly until the lion is trapped in their circle. With their spears held high above their heads and their shields stuck out in front, they sing to the lion, but it's no love song, that much I can tell.

"*Il oolmasin, eele, eele!*"

The words pile up on top of each other, carried along by a rhythm – it's a kind of eerie melody, calling up death. Their eyes are flashing as they sway around the lion like some mad kind of merry-go-round.

Ranan's beside me. His spear's ready, but me, I don't move. The *moran* is still pinned to the ground and he isn't moving, either. There's blood oozing from his shoulder where the lion's claws are nailing him down. The lion roars again and swings his head to show he's ready to finish off his prey, or anyone else who comes within reach.

The *moran* dance, holding the lion's attention, taunting him. It's exciting and cruel all at once. Then the lion turns once more to me and I wonder why. What is it about me? Is it my clothes, my colour, my lack of experience that has singled me out?

Then I realise – I'm the smallest one there.

The weak link in the chain. If he wants to escape, I'm the safest way out, and I want to step aside, give him an opening, but I can't. This lion has killed once, it might kill again, and there's something about the chanting that calls me in – says, "We are one. This is our destiny. A life will be lost."

As I stare into the lion's eyes, I hope it won't be my life.

~~~~~~~

There's a cry from the other side of the circle as someone jumps forward and grabs hold of the lion's tail.

It spins around, eyes flashing, mouth open, and I can see right into its pink throat, where the rumbling's coming from. All the time, the *moran* are chanting and closing in, drawing me in with them, hypnotising their prey.

Suddenly, a harsh movement breaks the rhythm as a spear is pushed into the lion's side. I don't see who does it, but it changes things – it can't be taken back.

The lion rises on his hind legs, paws clawing

the air as if he's trying to climb up into the sky, to escape from us. His face is twisted and his roar is so loud, I can feel it echo in my body, from my hair right down to my toes.

A spear flies from another part of the circle, then one more, and they're circling, stamping, chanting, closing in on him. His mane moves in waves, his eyes are liquid with fear, and his sharp yellow teeth glint in the sun as he roars, rises and staggers. Above the singing, I hear another sound. It's something I have never heard before – the sound of a large animal dying.

My spear drops out of my hand as I realise I don't want this. I need the lion to be all right, to run off into the forest and find his family, because families should be together. Things change forever when one member dies.

Suddenly, the roaring stops as the lion falls and lies silently on the ground. The *moran* move in to make sure he's dead and to check if their friend is still alive. The guy opens his eyes, but the lion's eyes stay shut.

Everything is quiet except for the faint echo of the last roar in my ears. It's as if this place has been closed off from the rest of the world and frozen as an image. We can never go back.

Ranan comes over to me and he's shaking, but his eyes are full of pride. "You looked in the lion's eye. He saw you were not afraid."

He is wrong – I was terrified and bewitched all at once. For one split second, it was just the lion and me. I can still feel his eyes burning into mine.

I push through the *moran* and kneel down beside the lion, placing my hand on his soft chest. There's no heartbeat, but he's still warm. I can feel the life that's been in him; see it draining into the dust through the spear wounds and leaking from his mouth. It's staining the earth red.

But stronger than that is the smell around me. It's like the scent of his strength and it's a thousand times stronger than the headdress in Odinga's shop – a smell I know I'll never forget.

twenty

As soon as the people of Enkasara see us coming, there's a lot of hooting and shouting.

The atmosphere is electric – like Christmas and birthdays and a football grand final, all rolled into one. The lion, dangling from spears by its tied paws, looks impressive. The *moran* are excited enough to burst. I just feel confused.

Women run up to hug Sempuku – the word has got around that he threw the first spear. We are quickly surrounded. So many bodies, so much noise. As usual, the kids are pushing in to see what I will do, although the lion's giving me some serious competition. For once I'm not the only attraction in sight.

Then Dad and Moses arrive. I can see Dad's

been running. He's all sweaty and looks like he's lost something. "Ash, are you okay?"

"I'm fine," I say, although I'm not really sure.

Dad's looking at me closely and I can't tell whether he's angry or proud or what. He's always saying how many protected animals are near extinction and we've just killed one – its body is still warm.

"What were you doing out there with the *moran* anyway?" Dad asks, but he seems more worried than annoyed.

"It's a long story, Dad. Besides, what happened out there is between me and the *moran*."

Saying this takes me by surprise, but I know that it's true. The details of the killing, and especially the ceremony that happened afterwards, are between the lion and the warriors. A secret business. Dad seems to understand.

"Okay, Ash," he whispers, "but what's this?"

He wipes something off my cheek with his finger and holds it up for us both to have a closer look. "Blood?"

I can see him looking me over to make sure it's not mine. Moses and Ranan look at Dad's finger, then back at me. Moses smiles. "It is lion's blood. It's the sign of a warrior. You should be proud."

Then Ranan says, "He looked in the lion's eyes. The lion saw Ash wasn't afraid."

"Like a true *moran*," Moses says with a broad smile. Which makes me wonder if that's what it means to be a warrior. I didn't climb the nearest tree like I thought I might. But, at the same time, I feel sadness – a lion is dead and I watched him take his last breath.

Dad just stares at the blood on his finger then back at me. Somehow, he seems to read my mind. "He killed a child, Ash. It had to be this way."

He's looking at me like he's trying to see right inside, and I want to help him, but I can't find the words. So he says it for me. "You've changed."

His eyes and his voice tell me I've changed, but in a good way, and it's as if things just got a bit more equal between us.

All around us, people are moving and there's cheering and waving. Preparations are already being made for the celebration, and I know it's big – the killing of a lion – but my head's too full of the smell, the roar, that final drop. I just can't get in the mood.

I feel a hand on my shoulder. I turn to see Sempuku, surrounded by the *moran*.

"Ashani. You must join the celebrations."

He's looking me in the eye, and there it is, that glimmer I thought I once saw – something that's telling me we're now friends. Ranan's beside me and the *moran* are smiling at us.

"Sure," I say. "We'll be right with you."

Sempuku leads the *moran* back into the crowd of cheering people. I look at Ranan. He's grinning at me. I know this is everything he wants. That for a Maasai this is as good as it gets and I can't help but share that feeling, too. Everyone's waiting for us to join them and celebrate our bravery. A dangerous animal is now no longer a threat.

One of the little kids grabs hold of the corner of my shirt and starts tugging at it, a mixture of respect and excitement in his eyes. I can see Sempuku and the other *moran* surrounded, and they're beginning to do that Maasai dance where they leap into the air as high as they can and seem to go into a trance. I can see why basketball coaches come out here to find new players – these guys could slam dunk their own sandals while they're still wearing them. It looks like fun, but, before I join them, I stand quietly for a moment and catch my breath. Because, although I wanted more than anything to feel what it's like to be a warrior, I now know it comes at a price.

twenty-one

The first thing I see when I open my eyes the next morning is the spear Sempuku gave me last night.

He told me to keep it as a souvenir and I grabbed it before he could change his mind. The only problem will be getting it through Customs.

Last night's dream comes flooding over me and I pull my sleeping bag up over my head to try to focus my mind. There is no jungle, just grasslands dotted with acacia trees. And there are the lion's eyes. He's coming closer, but this time it's different, I don't feel afraid.

In my dream, I kneel down and, as I put my

spear on the ground next to me, I hold out my hand. The lion walks right up to me and I can smell him and feel his soft mane between my fingers. I hear a voice. It's my mother and she is saying to me, "You're going to be okay."

And then it's gone. The dream slips away like sand through fingers. I put my hand on my throat to feel my necklace, the one with the lion's tooth, bought by my mother for a son who wasn't then born. And that son is me, and this necklace connects me to the lion, like it's been protecting me all along.

I turn round to see Ranan smiling at me, still rubbing the sleep out of his eyes. I want to ask him how he's feeling about everything, but I don't know where to start.

He nods towards the door and we get up quietly so as not to wake the others and head out into the bush for our early morning pee.

"Pretty good party last night, eh?" I say to Ranan as we pick a spot under the trees.

"Yes," he answers, giggling to himself.

"What?"

"I am thinking about Sempuku," he says laughing and having trouble peeing straight.

I remember last night – the *moran* in full flight, jumping up and down doing their dance, and Sempuku landing in a bucket someone left too close to their feet.

"Yeah, I know those guys like honey beer, but taking a bath in it is going a bit far."

We both crack up in front of an audience of monkeys who just shake their heads and chirp, like they think we're completely deranged.

"I am sorry you're going," Ranan says, pulling himself together.

"Me, too," I say, squatting on a rock under an acacia tree.

"We've learned many things together. Now we are brothers."

"Brothers?"

"Yes, brothers."

I try to imagine what the kids at school would say if I told them I had a brother. They'd say "yeah, right", because they all know me – at least they think they do. But, to Ranan, I really am a brother. We've done some amazing things together – learned to trust each other – and I guess that's what it's all about. Somehow, we've all been connected – Ranan, me and the *moran* – by everything that has happened. It's a bond that can never be undone.

"I have gift for you. Not here."

We walk back to the hut and everybody's up and having breakfast. Moses and Dad look like they could do with a bit more sleep after the celebration, but sleeping in is not really something you get to do in a Maasai village – unless you can doze through a troupe of toddlers using your stomach as a trampoline.

Ranan goes behind the screen and comes back holding a calabash – one of those milk containers that look like long wooden mangoes – but there's something different about this one. It's decorated all over with colourful beads and it has carvings burned into the wood. We take it outside to have a better look.

"I made it. It is my gift to you."

Ranan has carved a picture of a lion on it, just like ours – the way I want to remember the lion, strong and alive. But how could he have known?

"You made this before …"

Ranan smiles. "Before."

"Before" seems a long time ago – as if my life

has been divided in half by a great event and there's no looking back.

twenty-two

"Hello, Mr Porcupine."

Henry's back, and so are his bad jokes. The guy has a memory like an elephant. Ranan helps me carry all our gear to the car while Henry loads it up. Luckily, he packs everything really well. Otherwise, with his driving skills, it would be like driving through a battlefield, with spears and laptops as the weapons of choice.

"So, Henry. Take out any chickens on your way through?"

"Chickens? No chickens. This time I got me a big bird."

Henry sticks his hands behind his back like tail feathers, then he's off, running around in all directions, with his head sticking out in front of him like he's a couple of gigabytes short of a hard-drive.

Ranan's jaw drops about three metres, but

then suddenly he cracks up. "He is an ostrich."

"He's crazy, that's what he is," I say, laughing.

∿∿∿∿∿∿∿

Finally, it's time to go.

Dad and I have already said goodbye to just about everybody. The only two left are Ranan and Moses.

Dad and Moses start to say goodbye and their faces are a mixture of happy and sad.

"Goodbye, little brother," says Ranan.

I go to shake his hand, but he just kind of slides his palm across my palm, then holds on to my hand, not tightly, just enough not to let go.

"Goodbye, big brother," I say, grinning so hard that my back teeth are in danger of catching flies. I don't mind that he keeps holding on to my hand – it seems the right thing to do.

"Don't forget your Maasai family. We are always here."

Somehow, I hope that's true. That one day I'll come back to Kenya, to Enkasara, and the *enkang* will still be here. Ranan, too. I want more than anything for the Maasai to stay the way they are, but then who knows what the future will bring. I don't.

"Good luck with the initiation ceremony."

Ranan smiles. "It is not luck I will need for the *emorata*, only courage."

I'm not worried about that, because I know he's got truckloads of it. Hanging out with him I've learned a thing or two about being brave and, most of all, about being proud of who you are. Like the Maasai say, "A zebra cannot shed its stripes." So you might as well make the most of what you've got.

Ranan lets my hand go as the *moran* arrive. I'm surprised to see them, especially after all the celebrations, but they look in pretty good shape.

Sempuku steps forward. "We have come to say goodbye. In my country, men who hunt and kill a lion together will always be as one."

The *moran* are all behind him, a big wall of painted gleaming muscle, and me in my travel clothes and my short blond hair.

We look so different, yet we're now linked.

I hold out my hand and say, "Thanks." It's truly how I feel.

Sempuku puts his hand inside his *shuka*

and pulls something out. "For you," he says, placing it in my hand.

It's hair, but immediately I know. I lift it to my nose and smell it – it's a piece of the mane. The mane of our lion. I feel like he's with us – part of the connection that can never be undone.

We walk over to the car and Dad and I get in. It feels weird after a month of only walking. In a car, life just whizzes past, so if you blink you miss it. Then again, it can take you places that otherwise you might never see.

Ranan, Moses and the *moran* stand watching as we drive away. From a distance, they look like any group of Kenyans gathered on the roadside.

Except *their* faces are super-glued into my brain for eternity. Like pieces in my jigsaw that I thought I'd never find.

It's a lucky day for chickens. Henry manages to miss everything on the way back to Nairobi. He even misses a corner and lands us in a ditch. Luckily, a whole village turns up to help push us out or we would have had to spend the night. Funny how a place can look completely deserted, then out of the bush appears a village-load of people wanting to know what's going on. It's like our street on a hot Sunday afternoon when the ice-cream van turns up.

Nairobi seems huge after Enkasara, and way too noisy. It'll be good to be back in the hotel, to chill out a bit. Henry wanders in carrying the last of our gear. "Okay, Mr Porcupine. Time for Henry to go."

He shakes my hand and pats me on the head, in a way quite unbecoming to the brother of a Maasai warrior, but then he isn't to know. "Thanks for everything, Henry."

The next morning, Robert picks us up and drops us at the market.

Dad has lots of things he wants to get, but I don't feel like tagging along. "Why don't we split up for a while? I've got something I want to do."

"I don't know, Ash. I don't like the idea of

your wandering around on your own."

My dad! The same man who let me roam around the wilds of Maasailand carrying only a stick.

"Come on, Dad," I say, with a grin. "Last time I looked there were no lions roving around Nairobi market."

"It's not the lions I'm worried about," he says with a wink, but I can see he understands. "Back here in half an hour then."

"*Hakuna matata*," I say, slapping him on the shoulder.

"Ouch," he yells, squeezing the muscle on my arm. "Definite warrior material there."

I'm laughing as I take off, straight up to old Odinga's shop. He's sitting in the same place I saw him sitting last time – it's surprising nobody's ever confused him with a carving and tried to buy him as a souvenir.

"Ashani, you are back," he says, quietly rising from his stool. "And how was your journey?"

"Different from what I imagined."

"Ah, yes. Life is full of the unexpected, my young friend."

He follows me around, nodding, as I choose a couple of necklaces made of leather for some friends and a carving of a giraffe for Gran. It'll look good in her lounge, next to her wombat collection, and slightly more elegant, too. But what I really want is to go back into that room.

Odinga smiles and lights a candle. As soon as he pulls the curtain back, I can smell the scent of the lion's mane. My head buzzes with memories – the hunt, the *moran* painted in red ochre, the lion standing on his hind legs, trying for all he's worth to escape.

"Are you all right, young man?" Odinga's eyes are bright in the candlelight as he stretches out his bony old arm and puts his hand on my shoulder. "You are shaking."

"I went on a lion hunt."

"Why did you not say before?" asks Odinga, a quiet smile stretching across his face.

"I don't know."

But really I do. It's because it's not just a good story, it's too important to brag about.

Odinga passes me down the lion headdress, this time in a different way, as if he's crowning a king. He helps me put it on. It feels right, even if it's in some old shop in the Nairobi market and there are no Maasai around to see me wear it.

Before, I would have wanted to keep it, but now I know that this headdress doesn't belong in my bedroom. It's part of Africa, a part you can only carry in your thoughts.

I put my hand in my pocket and feel the piece of mane Sempuku gave me, and I know that I'm no Maasai warrior. I'm just a kid who has experienced something he only ever dreamed of, and learned truckloads along the way.

Suddenly, I realise that I wouldn't want to be anybody else – that I'm truly proud of who I am and where I come from.

For me, this is the true sign of a warrior. More than a headdress, or a drop of lion's blood on my body, or anything else. As we wait in the plane, my mind starts flicking back over the trip. A layer of Africa has slid into my mind, colouring my thoughts, mixed in with a little bit of sadness and a huge chunk of joy.

epilogue

Dad's hand is on my arm. "You okay, Ash?"

"Sure," I say, as the announcement comes over the intercom that we're about to take off.

"I know how you feel, but I've got something that will cheer you up."

I open my eyes. "What?"

"A fax," says Dad, holding it up in front of me.

"Who's it from?"

"The magazine."

"And?"

"They really liked the material I sent them

on Enkasara. They've got a new assignment for me."

"Cool! So, where are *we* off to next?" I ask him, giving him my best I'm-coming-with-you look.

"Well, I guess *we* are off to India. Rajasthan, to be exact."

"Rajasthan? *Raja*. Isn't that a king?"

Dad folds up the fax and puts it in his top pocket. "Rajasthan means 'the land of kings'. The whole place is dotted with palaces and forts. They want me to cover a camel fair in the holy city of Pushkar. I went there with your mum years ago. It's a big event – nomads and gypsies come from all over."

"Cool. It sounds like a fairytale, not a place."

"You'd better believe it."

I take a long look at Dad, who's got excitement written all over his face. He couldn't survive without me. He'll need someone to protect him from rampaging camels and to translate his jokes. And I'm the best man for the job.